Dear Teacher...

Letters From Modern-Day Monks

For more information on the The Bright Path, please visit:
www.TheBrightPath.com
Or contact:
publishing@thebrightpath.com

Cover Design: Yun-Shu Fang

Dedication

This book is dedicated to you who are on your own Holy Quest. Whether you have a niggling feeling somewhere deep inside that there is something more to life than you are currently experiencing, or a passionate yearning to seek the ultimate Truth, may the discoveries shared by the Ishaya monks on their own journeys, bring clarity, resonance, and inspiration.

Foreword

If you are one of those hardcore spiritual seekers, you might be able to relate to the passion of wanting to find the next book that will lead you to discover more about your inner path. You might also have a similar observation that, most if not all the books around spirituality, only refer to that one person's experience: the author, the guru, or the master of a particular tradition.

The truth is, this pure, pristine state of consciousness is not something that can only be experienced by those who dedicate their lives to meditating in the Himalayas, or those who were fortunate enough to be struck by spontaneous spiritual awakening. With a practice dedicated to Stillness and some consistent guidance, anyone can experience and live in that state of consciousness.

The Bright Path Ishayas are a group of modern-day monks who practice a Teaching, the sole purpose of which is to discover this truth. The Ishaya Tradition has honoured its lineage of delivering this truth from teachers to students since the beginning of time.

One of the intricate parts of being a direct student of The Bright Path Ishayas' teaching, is that we need to communicate with our Teacher regularly, (these days most often through emails) to share our exploration and experience of inner Silence and Stillness. As students, this allows us to stay very active in our practice and it enlivens our experience of the Silence within, continuously.

Some of the students' experiences and discoveries are so stunning that a few years ago, our Teacher, Maharishi Krishnananda Ishaya, started saving some of these emails in a folder. After years of saving them without having any idea of what purpose they may have until recently, my Teacher asked me if I would help compile these emails into a book (or perhaps, books).

Over the years, many people have suggested that my Teacher write a book of his own, but he recognised that it would be more powerful and inspiring for the world to read about the experiences of his students. What is unique about this book is that it is not just about a single guru's Teaching and experience, but rather, an account of many people's experiences of the same Teaching. The content is, therefore, a compilation of emails that were openly and authentically shared, from the students to their Teacher, without any intention or prior awareness of it being published as a book. The discoveries were real, genuine, and sincere, coming from the students' own direct experiences. If this many people can experience what has been shared in these emails, perhaps anyone can.

It is an incredible honour for me to be a part of the process of compiling this book. The level and quality of the experience from my fellow Ishaya companions is mind-blowing. For me, this is the true legacy of the Teacher and the Teaching. No amount of words one guru says speaks louder than the direct experience of Stillness that his or her students can convey. To me, that is the sign of a true Teaching of the One.

Priya Ishaya
Spain, 2023

Contents

Introduction...01

Part 1: The Homework...........................**03**

Chapter 01: The Attitude of Exploration................05

Chapter 02: Divine Will.................................33

Chapter 03: Here or Now?................................41

Chapter 04: Playing and Discovering.................53

Chapter 05: Does Awareness Feel?.....................71

Chapter 06: Beyond This Human Form.................95

Part 2: The Teaching.............................**111**

Chapter 07: The Ascension Practice...................113

Chapter 08: Playing with Awareness.................121

Chapter 09: Letting Go....................................133

Chapter 10: Happiness....................................145

Chapter 11: Oneness.......................................157

Chapter 12: The Path......................................167

Afterword..186

Glossary...187

Introduction

The emails in this book are written by The Bright Path Ishaya monks.

'Ishaya' is a Sanskrit term which literally means 'for highest Consciousness'. The Ishayas, in the context of this book, are an order of monks who have dedicated their lives to not only discover the highest Consciousness for themselves, but also to help others who have the same desire to do so. The Bright Path is the name of the organisation the Ishayas teach under.

The Ishayas teach a specific meditation technique called 'Ascension' to direct the awareness from the busy mind to the silence and stillness within. It includes an eyes-opened as well as an eyes-closed practice. Ascension means to 'rise above or beyond', and in the Ishayas tradition, it means 'to rise above or beyond the limitations of the mind'. Ascension consists of a series of techniques based on Praise, Gratitude and Love, which are known as 'Ascension Attitudes'. Within the context of our Teaching, we also use words such as 'ascending' or 'to ascend' which refers to the action of the practice. The term 'ascender' refers to those who choose to make Ascension their regular daily practice but have not taken on the commitment of becoming an Ishaya monk.

The desire to become an Ishaya monk is often driven by a deep aspiration to not only create a peaceful life, but to discover the ultimate Truth of who one really is - the infinite, boundless, eternal, immortal Self - which is the essence of everyone and everything. This is not widely or consciously recognised in the world today.

This desire leads to the inner Teaching of the Ishayas, also known as the Teaching of the One. The Teaching that there is only One existence, with the appearance of other. Just as many spiritual and mystical practices which are dedicated to

1

discovering the One within, the Ishaya Tradition has always endorsed and honoured the guidance of the Teacher to the students.

Maharishi Krishnananda Ishaya is the current Teacher of the Ishaya Tradition. In his style of teaching, he gives his students consciousness 'homework'. This includes many different approaches, observations, inspirations, and tools for his students to explore who they truly are and discover how to live life fully from there.

The students (aka the Ishaya monks) communicate regularly with their Teacher sharing their discoveries and experiences via emails. This is where the content of this book originated. None of the students writing these emails originally knew that their discoveries would be published and read by others, and this adds to the authenticity of their writings. Some of the emails are written by non-native English speakers or are translated from another language into English. You will be able to see different flavours, cultures, and ways of expressing the discoveries of the same Inner State. The Sanskrit names that you will see at the beginning and also as the signature at the end of most emails are the writer's Ishaya monk names, given to them by their Teacher.

Sometimes you will see the word 'God' being used. In the Ishayas' Teaching, this word does not have any religious connotations, nor does it refer to any form of an individual living somewhere above us in the sky. 'God' in our Teaching can also be called by many different names - it represents the universal force for good and only the good. People have their own concepts and terms for such a force; they might call it the Universe, Source, Silence, Stillness, Awareness, Tao, Nature, Truth, the One. It has been called many things in many places. Feel free to call it what you like and know that when you see the word 'God' in this book, you can translate it into the word that you believe represents the highest force for good.

Part One

The Homework

The first part of this book consists of a collection of emails sharing very specifically different consciousness homework that Maharishi has given out to his students.

Chapter One

The Attitude of Exploration

In the Ishayas' Teaching, especially between the dynamic of a Teacher and a student, there is a lot of emphasis on exploring, playing, and sharing various aspects of Consciousness. As inspiring as it is to hear the Teaching from the Teacher, there is another level of aliveness when the Teaching is applied with innocence and attentiveness by the students.

An attitude of exploration is everything on the path of awakening. To approach this inner path with any labels of 'good', 'bad', 'right' or 'wrong' is merely enhancing the belief of a separate 'self', the ego, so to speak. To approach this moment of discovery with the pure innocence of a child takes the seriousness out of the equation, a sense of wonder is restored, and our cup is empty enough to receive this very moment and everything it might have to offer, exactly as it is.

In one of the online meetings with Maharishi, he asked his students to share with him why being active in exploring the consciousness homework he gave them was important for their growth, based on their personal experiences and discoveries. The following emails are what Maharishi got in response.

Your Question

From: Sumati, United Kingdom
Date: December 09, 2021

So, your question… Why is exploring and sharing important to me?

When I'm active with my experience or a new way of approaching consciousness, my world expands. I'm a different person; inquisitive, playful, open, and resilient. If I'm sharing that with you, I unfailingly empty my cup leaving space for new experiences or seeing something I can let go of. I can't hold onto anything as a permanent truth because it's already gone. There's also no space for self-absorption. I desire to be empty and have life lived through me. That's the best way I know to do it. I actually feel lighter each time I share with you… if that's not a great incentive I don't know what is!

Lots of love to you,

Sumati

The Attitude of Adventure

From: Garuda, United Kingdom
Date: December 09, 2021

Hi Maharishi,

I'm currently loving the purity of my experience and just how simple and clear it is. I know it sounds funny, but I am either connected to Self or not. If I am not connected, then the mind goes berserk; but if I am, then the joy of nothing touching its presence is so amazing. It feels like all the 'fluff' is gone and there is only the choice.

Here is why I love the attitude of adventure…

I love that there is always more. I am always amazed by the magic, sacredness, wonder and purity of the experience.

Just by keeping it simple and by being as innocent as I can be, I am shown more and more revelations of Self.

What I notice is, this Eternal moment is endless and I am in total awe of the show.

Lots of love,

Garuda

What Keeps It Fresh For Me

From: Govinda, United Kingdom
Date: December 09, 2021

Hi Maharishi,

The things that have been a constant source of juice to go further for me are:

Actually moving to live the experiences that seem so 'advanced' way back when. Yet paradoxically not knowing that anything is changing and the 'ah-ha' moment when it appears as if some of the magic in the homework(s) is revealed.

Examples:

It does get easier and easier.

There is always more.

There is nothing to do.

The delicious paradox that looking to track any progress, frustrates it. The only way is to live in the experience of not thinking about living in the experience.

The immediate feedback is that if living is not easy and light, my focus is off. And the solution is so simple.

…there's more.

Peace love & joy,

Govinda

About Discovery

From: Hiranya, Norway
Date: December 09, 2021

I have an attitude of discovery on my spiritual path because it makes it more fun and interesting. What happens to my experience if I apply the homework? What can I find out about myself? Sometimes I discover more peace and joy, and sometimes I discover stuff that makes me cringe, like habits that aren't necessarily so pretty or flattering. But that can be quite fun, too! It is all about not taking anything too seriously and being open to growing. I like sharing these discoveries with my Teacher, too, because it often enlivens the discoveries further for me.

Love,

Hiranya

Inner Exploration

From: Mahadeva, United Kingdom
Date: December 09, 2021

Hi Maharishi,

You asked us why we explore. To some extent, it feels like I don't have a choice. I have had a curiosity and desire to understand since I was a small boy. Since meeting the Ishayas, it is as if these desires have become more and more refined, and the quest to know has been met halfway by a sense of something wanting to be known.

The experience of me and this separate thing has changed over the years to become simply an intrinsic part of my existence. Not so much a sense of me trying to get somewhere, but to allow what is to reach me. It is so obvious that 'I' can only interfere with that. When I am not engaged with 'me' and the mind, then what is there is just whatever is there, with nothing to judge if it is good, bad, better or worse.

The homework and subtleties you encourage us to explore bring flavour, texture, and vitality to the experience. To see where I am holding on, to discover where I can let go and to learn to not pick up in the first place make this fun, interesting, and has a profoundly positive impact on how I engage with life.

You shared a quote with me a few weeks back. "The most important thing is that the most important thing is the most important thing."* I love that!

Love, Mahadeva

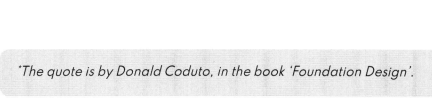
*The quote is by Donald Coduto, in the book 'Foundation Design'.

The Importance of Exploration

From: Nandasena, Mexico
Date: December 09, 2021

Hello, Maharishi,

The importance of exploration:

You know, for me, the idea of exploration got me totally interested since my First Sphere*. Right there I saw the potential of the Teaching and that it wasn't a static thing. Like knowing a new word, the word is always with the same meaning, but the Teaching was alive. It was something that I knew couldn't be put in a box of concepts and used on a daily basis. I knew that the exploration was for life.

Every moment I use the techniques is new and different from all other moments. Every time I discover something, I see that something inside me is different, and it is easy to see because my experience has changed, and with it, my truths, my beliefs, my points of view. With all of this my actions also changed. With this, my reality changed, and right there I knew I would never want to stop exploring because exploration leads me to discoveries, and sharing these discoveries with you gives me clarity. Everybody needs that clarity.

I love every aspect of the word 'explore'. At some point on this awesome path, I had some discoveries, like the experience that everything is inside me, not just that but everything is created from me, that everything is magic, and I am the magician and magic at the same time. With this experience, I wanted to go crazy with the amount of exploration I could have; and with this whole experience, I could not wait to share.

I have the perfect avatar to explore consciousness. I mean, why have a body and not use it? Hahaha.

I love you, Teacher.

The First Sphere - is the beginner's course to learn the Ascension practice, taught by qualified Ishaya Monks.

The Attitude of Discovery

From: Kali, United Kingdom
Date: December 09, 2021

Hi Maharishi!

In answer to your question about the importance of having an attitude of discovery, here's what I have on it:

I know what it's like to not have an attitude of discovery. I know what it's like to be alive in a body but not living… and I know that not having an attitude of discovery means not living.

From a young age I was taught that to be a 'spiritual' person in the world, you must be a warrior, and I believed this for a long time. When I met the Ishayas, however, I realised that I could drop all of this (it's hard work fighting your way through life as a warrior!) and instead, become an 'adventurer'. This is so much more fun, playful, exciting and expansive. Life still has challenges (and even times when we have to pick up the sword) but I would far rather explore my way through life and have an amazing adventure than fight all the time!!

I can see that without an attitude of discovery, I don't grow. I stagnate and I don't ever step out of my comfort zone. Fortunately, this happens rarely and when it does, life is pretty quick to throw something my way to snap me out of it!

Another cool thing I experience about having an attitude of discovery is that not only is it infectious to other people around us (and this is why sharing your discoveries is important) but it also feeds itself… the more I discover, the more I want to explore, and the more I discover… and so on.

I don't believe it's possible to live our heart's greatest desire without an attitude of discovery - it's critical!

I could go on! Thank you again!

Kali x

Why I Share My Discoveries

From: Maitreya, United Kingdom
Date: December 10, 2021

Ascension has given me an incredible enthusiasm for life and this enthusiasm spills over into sharing my discoveries with Maharishi. I used to hide my limitations, but I now enjoy seeing them. If I am honest, I often laugh about them (everyone else saw them years ago!).

Sharing what I discover is helpful because it keeps growth and stillness at the forefront of my attention. My connection with Maharishi is not only man-to-man but also magical and links me to the lineage*. I believe there is great power in that. A power that is activated by engaging my relationship with my Teacher.

By sharing my discoveries with him I experience a speeding up of my growth. If I am concerned about a situation and I share it, my concern is easier to surrender. If I discover something cool, like "love exists everywhere, always," I like to share the joy of such a cool discovery and sometimes it becomes more tangible and goes deeper into my experience.

I try to share most of what I experience with MKI. Good, bad, or ugly, it doesn't matter:

Good = great fun to share.

Bad = I get help with it and share the burden.

Ugly = I really get help.

If I want to grow but I don't share with my Teacher, it's like wanting to win an Olympic medal but not hiring a coach.

Love,

Maitreya

The Lineage - The Teaching of the Ishayas is an ancient Teaching passed down from Teachers to students. The Teaching is kept in its utter purity through thousands of years as it is an experienced-based lineage rather than a concept or a theory-based one. This Lineage is the backbone of the Teaching, and the Ishayas forever honour all the great Teachers (who are in essence, great students), who walked before us and preserve the purity of the Truth without compromise to this day so that we are able to experience it.

About Exploration

From: Dasahara, Mexico
Date: December 10, 2021

For me, the exploration is about LIFE, about how the perception of every moment transforms from shadows of grey into a delightful range of shining beautiful colours. It feels like that!

It looks like I am in "survival" mode if I'm not active in the experience, and at the moment I'm active again. LIFE is.

It amazes me to perceive how a slight shift in my attention transforms into divine in this moment. The infinite potential manifests in its grandiosity even in the middle of what could appear as immense suffering.

My passion is to live That, to witness That happening, to be That which is happening now.

And life is great. You go cruising… But then you put more attention on the Silence and suddenly, boom! Everything goes wild! Everything explodes in magnificence! The 'I' that has ideas, perceptions, protections, and limitations has no place here. There is nothing! And at the same time, there is the Totality of God.

Dasahara

Discovery, Exploration, and Passion...

From: Rajni, United Kingdom
Date: December 10, 2021

Hello Maharishi,

So, here's my take on discovery and exploration, passions, etc.

What I love about this path - The Bright Path - The Teaching of the One - The Teaching that there is Only God, is that it immediately connects me to an inner source - the unknowing. In this space, it is BIG, multi-dimensional, unchartered territory. I never get bored, because I have no idea what's going to show up and I LOVE that!

Don't get me wrong, sometimes I can get distracted and fragmented by the busyness of life, the stories coming from what appears to be a chaotic outside world. But when I allow myself to go inward and just be with it all, to simply watch and connect with this Teaching, there comes a moment (always!!!) when all the noise disappears. It's quiet. There is no separation.

Quite often, it's in this space I get clarity of the next step, my signpost, to where my path wants to take me. If I get stuck, I ask for help from my Teacher. And so, the discovery, exploration and experience continue! It never ceases to amaze me what unfolds. That's what I love about teaching. Putting all of that into creating something to help others.

For me it's yoga, it's deepening my love for life experience. I love hearing my students' own discoveries. So many times, I see faces light up, lives improve, and commitment to wellness and healthy living increase. Simple, powerful teaching with big endless results. My sole job - is to empty myself, be present, and let the universe live through me. It's awesome to be of service in this way.

Infinite love,

Rajni xxx

The Excitement of Exploration

From: Jaya, New Zealand
Date: December 11, 2021

Hi Maharishi,

The passion I have to explore - is my passion for life, my passion for connection with God, Source, the Infiniteness.

It's not a solution or an answer or trying to find something better, but celebrating what is right here, now.

It's vital for me to have this passion, this approach of excitement, because everything is instantly alive.

Sharing seems to be in all interactions, all conversations, and all expressions. Living it all.

One last thing, the passion and excitement for exploring this moment can often feel very simple, very embracing.

Love,

Jaya

Discoveries - Share

From: Shukri Devi, United Kingdom
Date: December 12, 2021

Discoveries from doing the homework and from going to online meetings etc. maintain the inspiration for me to keep going no matter what, and to be intrigued as to what more there is to experience. What else will I become? What is the purest version of this vessel?

It is inspiring because discovery is my direct experience. Not a concept, not something someone is telling me to do - but a direct experience, and there is no dialogue in that experience.

One of the most exciting discoveries is that it's really clear the more I put into the Teacher-student relationship, the quicker I am becoming free of the stuff. What I put in comes back 1000-fold. How honest I am seems to move mountains in my experience. Who I am now, compared with five years ago, even a year ago, is night and day. It's very cool to remind ourselves of that!

Life has a way of taking our attention and seeming to be very important with, for example, what appears to be huge responsibilities. But by applying what you say, I get to experience the actual Truth.

Shukri Devi

Discovery

From: Chandan, Germany
Date: December 12, 2021

Hi Maharishi,

The attitude of discovery and exploration is where the passion is and what makes my soul catch fire. Same thing with sharing those discoveries. There is eternal excitement to be had in discovering because there is no end to it. Also, it ultimately removes every obstacle or helps to transcend, or surrender, or see through a perceived obstacle.

There is just no quit in discovering.

So, in discovering, there is always more, and it seems to be the One's* driving force to go beyond it all. With an attitude of discovery, no limitation can ever win since there is an openness and a dropping of the insistence on what is believed to be real.

Chandan

*__The One__ - is another word that refers to the universal force for good; the Source, the Silence, the Stillness, God, the underlying reality of everything.

Why I Share My Experience & the Reason to Explore

From: Tapas, Germany
Date: December 12, 2021

Dear Maharishi,

To your question, what makes it so important to share my experience with you?

That's how I remembered your question (my short-term memory is rather poor), so I explored this first :).

· I can 'test' my experience for its Truth when sharing: Am I sharing shadows of words or my experience by using words, however inadequate?

· I re-experience it, though with a different flavour of the new & present moment.

· It opens my experience up to be seen: Therefore, if the experience turns out to be a shell of a concept, I trust you will show me.

· It's humbling.

· It's kick-arse enlivening.

· It's magical to connect; Something beyond the Teacher-student relationship is being awakened, as if the whole lineage takes part and starts celebrating and remembering.

- It's like hearing your favourite songs and falling in love with them evermore.

- It's like being switched on like a Christmas light and glowing like the star or angel resting on top of the tree.

- It's being attuned like a tuning fork to the ONE.

Now to your real question, which I listened to again just now :).

What makes it so important to discover & explore?

It seems the answers are in parts similar, which is wonderous. Yet there are some exciting additions:

- It keeps the explorations afresh & alive.

- It asks the question: What is unfolding right now, in this very moment! WOW - Look at that!

- It doesn't settle.

- It's falling in love with the present moment again & again, forever new.

- It's the very reason to choose & delight in the adventure of living.

Thank you for your questions, the real ones, and the imagined :).

With LOVE & GRATITUDE,

Tapas

Homework

From: Priya, Taiwan
Date: December 12, 2021

The reason why I love and continue to explore the Teaching/Homework is that it constantly allows me to let go of any sense of "I know". To explore, I have to let go of any sense that I know or own any experiences.

The experience is forever more alive not so much from what I gain from exploring but from letting go of any aspect of what I think I know. Exploring appears to be more of an inevitable state rather than an action when I am present.

Priya

Exploring and Discovering

From: Nagaraj, Germany
Date: December 13, 2021

Dear Maharishi,

You asked us to share our attitude toward discovering and exploring.

In my view, we must never stop.

What's the alternative? If we stop, we stop witnessing the wonder of life. If we stop, we go back into a wormhole, shackled by the chains of the ever-anxious mind instead of soaring like an eagle, fearless and high above the ground. From there we are able to see from horizon to horizon with an uninterrupted view, to witness life unfolding in its full majestic glory.

I've spent so much of my life in a wormhole, totally distracted by anxieties and worries about the future instead of seeing the abundance I was blessed with, let alone being able to appreciate it. By exploring the beauty of the moment I have a deep sensation of feeling alive, more so than I will ever be, surrounded by love, and blessed, carried and free from worry and concern. By exploring, I feel as if I am able to soar into the clear, fresh air.

It would be madness to stop.

Lots of love,

Nagaraj

Homework

From: Dharmaraj, United Kingdom
Date: December 15, 2021

Hi Maharishi,

This experience is all about discovery, it's all about not knowing what comes next, that is what keeps it alive.

There is freedom and also simplicity in that because I don't need to bring anything or add anything to this moment.

So, it is easy and fun until I get involved! Then the game becomes spotting that and letting go.

How does that change my life? It's the difference between living and just existing!

Love,

Dharma Raj

Passion

From: Manyu, United States
Date: December 15, 2021

The passion for me to explore and discover more lies in the way I get to experience life in many different ways.

As the Silence remains forever the same, the world is the opposite. It is constantly changing, shifting, moving, like a wild river... sometimes slow, sometimes deep, sometimes fast and never the same. To be given the jewel of Life, to be given the ability to experience existence itself is amazing. To be given a second chance at life, through the Ishayas, is a great blessing. To be able to experience the Infinite Ascendant* is the most precious gift of all.

The sacredness that has been shown to me, creates the fire and desire to constantly and continually follow this Path, follow my Teacher, and do my best to remain innocent and humble to what God is giving to me now.

Love,

Manyu

The Ascendant - is a word created by the Ishayas, as a neutral term to refer to the universal force for good; the Source, the Silence, the One, God, the underlying reality of everything.

Chapter Two

Divine Will

The question of "free will" is often raised in the context of spirituality. Is there a "free will" or is it all part of the Divine Plan? Rather than giving a direct answer, Maharishi asked his students to explore the idea of 'my will', 'free will' and 'Divine Will' from their direct experience of resting in the Stillness.

Your Question on God's Will

From: Tapas, Germany
Date: May 31, 2022

Dear MKI,

Before ascending, I was probably the most impatient person. You couldn't tell me a thing twice because my memory is such that I store everything down to the last detail the first time I hear/see something, and I tended to get bored or annoyed hearing it a second time.

Now I literally can hear something 1000 times and it still is fresh with a new breeze of wisdom, discovery, insight and magic. I can also repeat something many times without feeling I repeat myself - win-win :).

In last Sunday's meeting, you asked if we have a sense 'that everything brought to us is absolutely in keeping with God's Will', and the perfection of all that is brought to us. I absolutely do. No doubt about it. It overwhelms me sometimes with the love and joy of what God is experiencing through me, the essence gifted by God, my resilient and strong vessel. It keeps me glued to life to experience all there is to experience. I feel beyond blessed to even have the experience of living. So, what a great question. Thank you.

With love,

Tapas

It's All Unfolding Perfectly

From: Maitreya, United Kingdom
Date: May 31, 2022

Hi Maharishi,

I just wanted to write to say how strong this knowing is within me.

Everything that has ever happened was Divine Will. There is no other way, it could not be anything else. Everything I have experienced, done, etc., has been an unfolding of divinity. It's amazing. No one has ever done anything wrong! I have never done anything wrong! Wow! I feel so complete. As if I am here to experience and enjoy life, to play and explore, but all is well on every level. It's a very content and wonderful thing to know.

Love,

Maitreya

Being One - God's Dance

From: Tapas, Germany
Date: June 03, 2022

Dear Maharishi,

I woke up this morning,

with this Knowing.

I was dreaming,

and all of it are aspects of 'me'.

Therefore now that I am awake,

not dreaming, yet dreaming,

all of that I am experiencing, seeing, feeling,

are aspects of that same 'me'.

It's the wave of the ocean

that is experiencing itself.

It's grace for the crest to crash

into the ocean to merge. For a moment...

for eternity...

or any timeless space in between.

It is God,

experiencing itself.

It's God's dance…

the wave, the crest, the ocean,

being One.

With love,

Tapas

This Moment

From: Nagaraj, Germany
Date: June 02, 2022

Dear Maharishi,

I missed the last teachers' meeting because I was on a bike trip. We intended to watch the replay a few days ago but somehow accidentally ended up watching an older talk of yours. In that talk, you spoke about how this moment is so so precious as the universe had to go through millions of permutations to bring us this special experience.

I needed to ponder what you said for a few days. At the back of my mind, I heard this voice saying, 'but what if it's all just total coincidence?' My mind was challenging the idea of a master plan.

Today it hit me. If we are the smartest thing in the universe, then everything is probably just unfolding by chance and accident. But if we accept there is a higher intelligence at play, then all we need to do is accept that everything is just perfect the way it wants to be. Just like a dog accepts its master's commands, knowing it's for the best.

Now what I know, and constantly experience through Ascension, is a deep understanding and acceptance that a greater intelligence is at play, and that makes Amor Fati* so much easier to embrace because in the end, everything that is given to us is ultimately for our own benefit.

As always, I thank you.

Nagaraj.

*__Amor Fati__ - is a stoic Teaching. Amor Fati is a Latin phrase and literally translates as "Love of Fate". It found its most explicit expression with the German philosopher Nietzsche, who made love of fate central to his works.

"My formula for greatness in a human being is amor fati: that one wants nothing to be different, not forward, not backward, not in all eternity. Not merely bear what is necessary, still less conceal it—all idealism is mendacity in the face of what is necessary—but love it." - Nietzsche, 'Ecce Homo: How One Becomes What One Is', chapter title "Why I am so clever".

Amor Fati became one of the approaches that Maharishi has his students play with in moving towards surrender and embracing Divine Will: to not merely bear what is necessary but love it.

Chapter Three

Here or Now?

Being in the here and now is often referred to, not just in the context of spiritual practices, but also in the modern-day approach of being present and not getting caught up in past memories or future worries. 'Here' and 'now' are being talked about as a joint concept so much that most people think they are the same thing.

Maharishi suggests that 'here' and 'now' are actually two different approaches to being present. He asked his students to pick between a 'here group' or a 'now group' and play extensively on the approach they have chosen and see what they discover.

The following collection of emails consists of students sharing specifically about the 'here' or the 'now' group they have chosen, as well as general discoveries on living a life fully in the present.

Share Homework

From: Divya, Mexico
Date: December 13, 2021

I want to share what I am discovering with the new homework.

I chose to be now and live God at all times.

I am also observing how the attention was out looking for something every time I chose; it was like looking for a reward, and I had no peace. Immediately with the homework, it was easy, and for now, the experience seems to be at peace.

Thanks for your guidance and love.

Divya

Only One Job

From: Jayatsena, Sweden
Date: November 04, 2022

There is only one thing to do, and that is to be here now.

I do understand why, because here and now there is nothing that needs to be done, all is well and beautiful. I get glimpses that 'nothing moves'. It is very fleeting, but the essence/flavour lingers and is there to show me that I just keep playing.

It is such a gift; I get tears in my eyes when I follow the feeling of gratitude and wonder. The question "what have I been doing all this time then?" is a good one. Trying I guess is the answer. Trying to do something right, something better, something to be freer in this process of awakening. But again, the experience of being unbounded awareness and divine presence really seems to be no process, it just is. And yet my mind makes a process of it many times, does a little timeline and binds me to it. But every moment I just let go and be free, then I am free. Haha. Hilarious. Walking, running, working around in circles to just arrive here. Magic.

So cool!

Peace!

Jayatsena

Here and Now

From: Nagaraj, Germany
Date: January 03, 2022

Dear Maharishi,

Happy New Now!

I wish you all the best for 2022. It will be a vintage year. I can feel it already.

You asked us to play with Here and Now. As I was in the Here group, I have switched over to play with Now. Being in the Here group was relatively easy. Especially your tip "just to be where my legs are" has made it easy to remember to be Here.

Now is trickier. However, I have just had a realisation.

I attended a motorbike track training course last year. They taught us to treat the footrests as a gauge. Especially in the wet, the footrest will kick out if you are about to lose the rear end. Having a gauge can be such a useful tool. There are a few more all over the bike which they also taught us about.

Aren't our senses a gauge to help us stay in the Now? How often are we actually aware of our senses? At the best of times, we may be aware of one, sometimes not even that. I am now using my senses to remind me to be in the Now, because only in the Now is it possible to be aware of the senses. It's impossible to smell yesterday's ocean or hear tomorrow's birdsong. Or feel the next minute's gust of wind blow over your skin.

Only Now can you truly experience what it's like to be alive. Just by having your senses switched on. And if your senses are switched on and active, it's as if you have become a walking, breathing and living antenna that connects you with the universe.

Safe travels!

Nagaraj

Way to Freedom

From: Meera, United Kingdom
Date: January 20, 2022

Hi Maharishi,

I've found for many years that all the so-called 'bad stuff' has been the most growthful in my experience. I have always been so grateful for those things and the people who push me.

Pain has been one of the biggest teachers for me as you know and has always made me pay attention because it has, in the past, been so uncomfortable that you just can't stay holding on!

Relationships too, especially in my family, have been so hugely transformative. As you said, I wouldn't exactly choose to repeat the lessons learnt! But I also wouldn't have it any other way.

My comfort zone has been ripped apart again and again and I'm super grateful for this.

I'm also grateful that I appear to not battle with what arises now. It's so clear that everything comes to me to help me wake up, so I gladly welcome it in with open arms. Sure, I occasionally close my eyes, look away and brace for impact!!! But I soon realise there isn't one and I turn to face everything and bathe in the gentle embrace of this moment when I fully show up for it.

The here-and-now homework still reveals a more alive and vibrant experience of this moment, where laughter frequently bubbles up and a mischievous twinkle in my eye becomes contagious for those around me! :)

Life unfolds in glorious multicolour hues, and I fall in love with this moment again and again...

Love,

Meera xx

Asleep

From: Nagaraj, Germany
Date: June 09, 2022

Dear Maharishi,

I had an uncomfortable realisation yesterday about how often I am not here, i.e. not being fully present and attentive to this moment. I caught myself looking out of the window and then, with a startle, I realised that I wasn't in the room. I was miles away, occupied in thought. I simply forgot. But realising that I am not here right now is probably an important step forward. Just like recognising one's own mistakes is the first step of learning, because you can then avoid them in the future.

In that moment of looking out of the window, I also had another realisation. I suddenly understood that when I am not present, I literally miss the whole point of being alive, just like falling asleep during a film means you miss the climax at the end (happens to me all the time by the way). There is nothing wrong with being asleep, except you miss the whole point of the film. There is also nothing wrong with not having seen the Grand Canyon or climbed a mountain or ridden a bike across a continent, etc., etc., etc. - but once you have had such an experience, you would not want to miss it, and it will stay with you for probably the rest of your life because it acts as a constant reminder of what it means to be alive.

I so, so love that quote from MSI* about life being meant to be lived in eternal bliss. I now also recognise, more so than ever, why life is meant to be lived consciously. Not because it's more fun and everything is just a little bit easier, it's actually the whole point of being alive. To bear witness to the universe's magic show and to marvel at the interplay of literally everything as it unfolds in this very moment, because otherwise, we are practically asleep, missing the point of what it means to be born entirely.

Thanks to Ascension, I know how to choose for the silence, and that provides me with the ability to return. As long as I recognise when I have left this moment, I can always come back. What a powerful tool we have! It's like flicking a light switch... Lights off: sleep, lights on: wakey, wakey, with instant illumination. Coffee is served.

Have a fabulous day!

Nagaraj

M.S.I. (Maharishi Sadasiva Isham) is the Teacher of Maharishi Krishnananda Ishaya. One of M.S.I.'s most used quotes from his book "Ascension!" is, "Life is meant to be lived in Eternal Joy, Infinite Freedom, Unconditional Love and Unbounded Awareness. Any other life is utterly missing the point of being born human."

Peace Prevails

From: Maitreya, United Kingdom
Date: November 30, 2022

Hi Maharishi,

The last few days have been some of the happiest and most peaceful of my life. Being in Edinburgh has been wonderful, but going back to my home city has also presented me with some old grooves*.

A few days ago, I decided to do the 'now' homework. At around that time, I seemed to drop a lot of the stress around uni work, managing my life, etc. It's like I have fallen in love with stillness again. It's so important, so pervasive. The ins and outs of life are just happenings that come and go but happen within presence, not instead of it.

I am loving being alive, primarily so I can experience presence in a human body. I often laugh for no reason and life is great!

Love,

Maitreya

---

*__The Grooves__ - is a term we use in the Ishayas' Teaching, referring to the limiting concepts and beliefs that we've accumulated throughout our lives, which in time engrave in our belief system and form our reality and identity the way we perceive them.

NOW

From: Nagaraj, Germany
Date: January 20, 2023

Dear MKI,

Yesterday, whilst cooking, I was reminiscing about all the great experiences I have had in my life - riding a motorbike to Melbourne, drinking Mojitos on a Havana beach, hitchhiking across Israel... Then I realised how removed I actually was from those events. I am grateful for everything I have been able to experience to date as it has allowed me to get to this present moment but despite how amazing those events might have been, they are no longer alive. It feels as if I was observing them from the sidelines. I didn't even feel like the main protagonist. Anybody could have had those experiences and I could just as easily read their account. I doubt it would be less engaging.

The only time an experience is truly alive is right now. That's why it's so so important to be attentive to what's happening right here, right now. This is where life unfolds and where we as human nervous systems are able to consciously experience what it means to be truly alive. You blink and you miss it, that's why it's so important to have the tools we have. They are like an Uber to Now, on speed dial.

Lots of love,

Nagaraj

Chapter Four

Playing and Discovering

In most of the meetings and discourses with our Teacher, he will give us small games and tools to play with in our exploration of consciousness. This leads to discoveries of different aspects of the Silence and the refinement of our ability to stay attentive and aware. Most of all, they keep the journey fun and alive.

It is like being in a cosmic sandbox playing with different toys to explore the cosmos within. The paradox of being on a path of awakening is that there is actually no goal, no objective. This is not a linear path that eventually leads to an endpoint, which we might call awakening, enlightenment, self-realisation, you name it. It is simply a recognition: that which we seek already resides in the living state of experiencing, Now. All the guidance and approaches are simply to get our attention to Now.

This chapter contains a mix of emails all referencing miscellaneous homework and the discoveries that have come from exploring them.

Fully Enjoying Life

From: Brihas, Germany
Date: December 10, 2021

Dear Maharishi,

Playing with Amor Fati* keeps on changing my dynamic with life. It's like I get more and more pulled into life because it is so rewarding with all this aliveness. Withdrawing from life feels so incredibly boring now. All I want is to fully take advantage of life and play fully. It's like I am experiencing the Treasure of being alive more and more.

The God homework** is also mind-blowing. It has totally transformed my relationships. Instead of others being separate individuals that have an impact on my individual part - everybody is now part of the One affecting me the same way as every other aspect of creation - as a gift to get to know myself more. It is really incredible to see that probably everything I would see in the other person is only my own projection.

What I love so much about exploring consciousness with your homework is that it turns life instantly into an exciting adventure. Instead of trying to get through life, I can enjoy the discovery of amazing new insights and experiences in consciousness. It is so fulfilling on its own that the rest of life doesn't seem so important anymore.

That mainly means there is no reason to be serious about anything anymore. Life becomes more like a dance and an infinite win-win situation, because I either have pleasant experiences to enjoy or unpleasant experiences that teach me how to enjoy life even more.

Living like this makes the flow of Magic so obvious. It reveals that everything follows a perfect plan that I will never be able to understand, but I can let it unfold and enjoy all the benefits.

Thank you for your amazing guidance. I love you.

Brihas

Amor Fati - is a stoic Teaching. Amor Fati is a Latin phrase and literally translates as "Love of Fate". It found its most explicit expression with the German philosopher Nietzsche, who made love of fate central to his works.

"My formula for greatness in a human being is amor fati: that one wants nothing to be different, not forward, not backward, not in all eternity. Not merely bear what is necessary, still less conceal it—all idealism is mendacity in the face of what is necessary—but love it." - Nietzsche, 'Ecce Homo: How One Becomes What One Is', chapter title "Why I am so clever".

Amor Fati became one of the approaches that Maharishi has his students play with in moving towards surrender and embracing Divine Will: to not merely bear what is necessary but love it.

The "God Homework" is a reference to the homework that Maharishi gave to his students on "seeing everyone as God". It is an approach of seeing everything and everyone in creation as all Divine and recognising that nothing is separated from anything else.

The Homework

From: Rudra, United Kingdom
Date: December 13, 2021

Hi Maharishi,

For me, the most exciting thing has always been the possibility of experiencing the Silence continuously in daily life. There was never much interest in only experiencing Silence in certain restricted moments during closed-eye practice.

Once the realisation came that this was not only possible but easy with the guidance received, then playing with the homework became the most magical opportunity to experience the One in every waking moment.

It seems to come down to priority. What is the priority in every waking moment?

The One, or something else?

To experience 'This' now is pure magic and contentment, there is no second best. The homework is a wonderful way to keep that alive but also to explore, expand and solidify the experience more and more.

Rudra

Playing with the Homework

From: Matri, Mexico
Date: December 16, 2021

Dear Teacher,

For me playing with the homework is a great gift, not only
for me, but it also allows me to see the beautiful impact it
has on the people near me and those I interact with.

It helps me to see so clearly where I put my attention or
where I can't let go, but mostly it's showing me that there
is no limitation to me playing big. There are of course
moments when I can forget this and it's beautiful to have the
homework as a reminder!!

I'm feeling very grateful to you, Teacher, and to this
Teaching, for showing me how to live fully!!

With so much love and gratitude,

Matri

Hi

From: Sevaka, United Kingdom
Date: December 19, 2021

What is working for me is the "Seeing everybody as God" homework*; it makes my experience a lot more gentle and soft. I'm a lot more welcoming of my experience generally in the world because people make up such a huge part of that. This has been an important discovery for me.

If I extend that to God being in absolutely everything, then that brings a lot more consistency to my experience. It was really helpful to hear what you said on the call today, Maharishi, about even seeing your special thoughts** as God. For some reason, I never thought to do that before. It completely changes the game and takes a lot of the seriousness out of things and kind of makes the whole thing about special thoughts hilariously funny!

This also has the effect of diminishing any distinction between an inside and an outside. In that respect, I find this very similar to the living IN God homework, which I also love. If absolutely everything is God, then how can there be any sense of separation?

There have been some big changes and I'm excited to see what lies ahead.

Much Love,

Sevaka xx

*Seeing Everyone as God Homework - *An approach of seeing everything and everyone in creation as all Divine and recognising nothing is separated from anything else.*

**Special thoughts - *is a term used to describe the kind of thoughts which seem particularly big or reoccur in someone's experience. Rather than thoughts that come and go easily, the special thoughts appear to be easier to grab onto and get dragged along by.*

Homework, Highest Desire

From: Philip, Sweden
Date: July 11, 2022

So! I'm going to try approaching the homework by playing with one for a week and then updating you about it and then going on to the next one. I've tended to play very intensely with it right away as I get it, but then I've sort of forgotten it or done it sparingly until I'm reminded again….

Now I've made lists that I've put up above my desk so I can see them every day.

- To be clear: what do I want more than anything? It seems the phrasing can be different at times, but I know it's this: to become one with God. I know this is my highest desire. And it's a bit scary to actually write it because I don't know what's coming. So, then I'm gonna Amor Fati that!

- What does the best version of me look like: loving, generous, giving, playful, forgiving, inspiring, present, empty, open, creative. The exploration continues on how to live that. But I noticed just now that when I rest in Silence, I want to give and serve - give the gifts I'm being given.

- I realise that I love writing to you, it puts me back into connection with Source.

Lots of love and gratitude to you,

Philip

Homework Update

From: Philip, Sweden
Date: July 21, 2022

Hello Teacher!

So last time I wrote to you I said I was going to play with one Homework at a time. Funnily enough, it seems now that I've been playing with all of them at the same time these last 10 days.

These two have been most prominent:

How can I give more today: I often feel I'm giving and I love doing that. This homework sparked an unexpected resistance! It made me see where I'm NOT giving when I CAN. It's highlighted the crossroads where it's up to me to make an active choice. It's made me aware of the freedom to give at any given moment.

Now that I'm writing I realize I've been seeing it like a fun game. It's like a bell goes off that says "Here's a chance to play, be attentive and give more" - compared to if I'm in 'autopilot/normal' mode. That makes all the difference.

I've made many choices to give more, although it may seem small - like talking to someone in the street and laughing together, saying hello to strangers, joking with and encouraging girls selling cookies on the street, making initiatives with family. Actually, a lot of giving seems to be through making people laugh! To me, it seems almost like this homework could be translated to: 'Have more fun!'

It's also shown up in conversation, to be more open, more curious, and more generous. So yes, this goes hand in hand with being the greatest version of myself. It's an active play.

Seek first the Kingdom of Heaven*: This has made me really aware of where I'm not putting God first, where I'm not making the choice for Peace most important. And it's giving me a very active choice: Do I prioritize This or that? It's like a lie detector that goes off. Bzzzz.

Thank you! I realize again how clarifying it is to write to you.

Lots of love,

Philip

---

*Seek first the Kingdom of Heaven - not to be taken in a religious context but what it literally means: the Kingdom of Heaven is at hand, seek it first, seek it now. Not to postpone it till another moment (perhaps after we die). It is an Ishaya's priority to discover the experience of Heaven within, in this present moment.

From Asha: Sharing Homework

From: Asha, Brazil
Date: July 31, 2022

Morning from Brazil! Let's go:

1. My best version*: is the still version. The version with no thoughts. The version when I am whole with everything. The version that is complete and there is nothing missing. The Silent version. The version with no me... the here-and-now version.

2. How to be always like that? I just keep on going with this Path. It is getting better, easier, more fascinating, more magical, and more enjoyable by the minute. And I know there is more. My arms are open to life and to what the Universe presents to me. I am open and willing to play my role.

3. What is my purpose: to wake up and to share with humanity how to do it. There is nothing more fulfilling in life than that. And while doing it, Creation is happening through me. I have never been so productive and happier in my life. I have never been so grateful for this Path and this life opportunity. There is magic and abundance everywhere. There are presents and learnings everywhere. It is like God is talking to me all the time via everybody and everything. I love it.

4. Talking from Silence**. Allowing the Universe to speak via me. It is unbelievable. I am playing with this homework, and I hope I never forget to do it. I can also write from Silence. And it is fascinating as well.

Love, Asha

*Maharishi once gave out homework asking his students to write and describe what they perceive as the greatest version of themselves.

Talking from the silence - is a homework that focuses on practising consciously resting in the state of inner silence as the foundation to engage in any speech or action.

August Update

From: Śivananda, Australia
Date: August 18, 2022

Dear Maharishi,

So… two weeks into my commitment to speak from silence*. The main thing I've noticed is that it's not that different. In other words, I think that is what I do most of the time. My work with clients is definitely like that. My best advice comes from the silence, and their experience (and mine) is that I am very present with them.

My favourite story of speaking from silence happened a few days ago. We arrived at the resort for a week's skiing, unpacked the car and carried everything to the lodge. Then I drove the empty car a couple of kilometers down to the car park.

On the way, I saw a guy walking down the road carrying his skis and a boot bag. So, from the silence, I pulled over and said, "hey mate, want a lift?"

He was very grateful… he thought he was in for a long walk after a hard day's skiing carrying all his stuff after he'd just missed the bus.

After I parked my car and started walking back up the hill, I thought perhaps someone would give me a lift. So, I stuck out my thumb. Two minutes later, who should pull over but Rene, the ambo (the guy I had given a lift to). He was thrilled to be able to return the favour.

I was also very impressed... normally Karma takes longer than 5 minutes to come back!

With love,

Śivananda

Talking from the silence - is a homework that focuses on practising consciously resting in the state of inner silence as the foundation to engage in any speech or action.

Homework - No Complaining!

From: Rajni, United Kingdom
Date: September 22, 2022

Hi Maharishi,

Oh, have I been having fun with this one!

What strikes me is that as soon as you have awareness of the complaining it does the following:

- Immediately helps me to recognise that I'm complaining - alarmingly too much one feels.

- It's always coming from the past or the future.

- It feels like resistance.

- Gives immense joy when you can let it go.

- Provides space to feel joyful and literally laugh about how ridiculous it is.

- Enables me to tap into this moment even more so and stay in it.

I had to share this homework with the morning ascenders group in the UK and it triggered a wave of interest, fun and laughter - it was awesome to watch. Many of them started to recognise different ways we complain - in our thoughts, words, and actions.

Thank you so much - I will continue to play with this - love it!

Love & Peace,

Rajni xxx

*The 'No Complaining' Homework - is an approach which focuses on becoming more conscious of not engaging in any complaints or instigating them, externally as well as internally.

Chapter Five

Does the Awareness Feel?

Emotions, feelings, and sensations rise and fall in our day-to-day experiences. One of the areas that many spiritual seekers have been exploring forever is the relationship between such movement and Silence/Stillness.

When students are struggling with emotions and feelings (particularly those that are perceived to be negative ones), our Teacher often says, "That which is aware of sadness/anger/depression, isn't sad/angry/depressed." The feelings might appear to rise; but who we truly are is that infinite Awareness, aware. We are aware of our feelings and emotions, but we are not our feelings or emotions.

In this homework, Maharishi asked his students to explore the following question, "Does the infinite Awareness that you are, feel?"

Investigation

From: Ishani, Mexico
Date: January 26, 2022

Hola!

So, I LOOOOOOOOOOOVE this investigation. It is SUPER EXCITING to be aware of the feeling thing.

LOVE IT!

I've been suspecting this for some time now; I thought I might be a little crazy, but now I feel I'm not!

It's like if I'm super aware, like really HERE, I can be sensitive and aware of the feelings. I can notice the feelings, detect them, BUT I don't feel them.

This is something which when I heard it from you the first time shocked me so much, and it's something I remember frequently. Something that always pulls me back to this moment - "That which is aware of the sadness is not sad". I feel that apparently, it applies to all the wonderful rainbow of emotions.

Now, with this investigation homework, it's like the whole cosmos went CLICK!

So far, it appears that if I'm truly present, truly aware, out of 'the story', I can be aware of the emotions like I'm aware of the weather or the squirrels... I can see them, I can recognise them, but I don't feel it in my being, I don't feel them like they're 'mine'.

Oooooobviously there are moments when I do believe

I'm feeling this or that, but I totally recognize that in those moments I'm making it about being 'me', a separate individual who can be hurt or applauded. And it's like I'm entering 'human mode'. Totally fake mode.

And by fake, I mean illusion.

It's like this world is an illusion, the stories, the boundaries, the problems, the drama, the intense feelings... Yes, I can feel it all if I'm in 'illusion mode', then when I remember, I wake up to reality and there's nothing here. It's like none of this has ever truly existed.

Exactly like when one is asleep, dreaming and waking up.

In this reality, there's no "I feel this or that" it's like a suspended, still, eternal void without any movement. A suspended peace and contentment with no subject to qualify the experience, but just the experience, still, unmovable, sturdy, and weightless peace.

And it feels like 'the normal', natural, safe state of consciousness.

No stories attached, no character.

Just stillness.

When I forget and get involved in the dream, it doesn't matter. No big deal. It's so ephemeral that it dissolves into the greatness of the moment. And there's no fault or mistake, there's no one to blame because apparently, it doesn't matter.

I'm sooooo in love with this exploration.

It's so exciting to be aware and to discover more.

Thank you for the homework. It's amazing how everything is here but still, one needs the Teacher to make this insightful movement in our attention.

I love you.

Ishani

Awareness

From: Manyu, United States
Date: February 07, 2022

Does radiant awareness feel?

In my experience, it does not appear to be so. So, no.

Awareness is more than a feeling. All feelings and emotions come and go. Conscious awareness does not become the object (the feeling).

It seems to me that Awareness has this infinite flexibility to be aware of anything or everything, experiencing it, without becoming it. Awareness never loses its pureness.

Peace,

Manyu

To Feel or Not to Feel...

From: Kali, United Kingdom
Date: January 29, 2022

Hi Maharishi,

Hope this finds you well in the run-up to a LIVE retreat!

I just wanted to let you know how I'm doing with one of your latest questions: does the pure awareness that you are, feel?

I've been playing with it all week and it has been fantastic. I would go so far as to say it's a life-changing question!

My answer so far, is that it would appear that no, the pure awareness that I am does not feel (there is no 'feeler' to 'feel').

I love this question for many reasons... Firstly, it's shown me that whenever I get caught up in a feeling, it means, simply, that I am not fully aware. I knew and experienced this previously, but I love the particular angle of this question and the fact that there is no wiggle room in it!

I've found it useful also as a baseline when around others, particularly those who are on a mission to make it all about what they 'feel'.

To me, this Teaching has never been about denying feelings, pushing feelings away, or not listening to feelings (although I think we can end up doing that if we approach the Teaching conceptually, or try to run before we can walk with certain issues), but I see there are levels way beyond 'what we feel'.

Yes, I have to 'do' work around emotions to help me access the Teaching more, and I've done plenty of trauma work too… Perhaps, I will always need these things, but I've never seen them as a replacement for a Teaching that is so beyond all these things. Surely, pure awareness can never be angry, sad, or even happy (from an emotional level)… it's almost funny!

And yet, this Teaching has been a gift in allowing me to feel more! I used to be so disassociated and terrified of my emotions that I was wandering around in a permanent state of shock. Ascending has thawed that… enabled me to see emotions for what they are, to step through and beyond them to something that feels far more 'real'… in the form of awareness. It's so ironic that I perhaps feel more than ever before, and yet… those feelings are just energy moving through.

Allowing this has allowed me to live more fully… experience the amazing tapestry of life and savour the gifts of joy, grief, rage, without attachment, because the experience of God is so much bigger than those tiny, fleeting parts of the ocean of awareness.

Anyway, I don't know if any of that makes sense… I will keep playing!

Kali x

Does the Ascendant "Feel"?

From: Bharati, United States
Date: February 07, 2022

Maharishi,

To answer this question, I would say No. 'Feeling' is a human construct, probably originally describing physical sensations (hunger, heat, pain, etc.) and then in more recent years, psychological descriptors for vague sensations within the body that appear connected to thought & vice versa.

Yet the Ascendant may have experiences of its own. I mean, all is a part of the whole and what is the whole? What exactly is that which we call Brahman or consciousness?

What is this feast of everything, and nothing? Of here, and limitless? Of this silent luminescence?

So perhaps my best answer is simply: I don't know.

Bharati

The Ascendant - is a word created by the Ishayas, as a neutral term to refer to the universal force for good; the Source, the Silence, the One, God, the underlying reality of everything.

Sharing

From: Dasahara, Mexico
Date: February 07, 2022

Hello Teacher,

I have been playing with your question of "if the Consciousness feels". Right away, my answer was "No", but anyway, I wanted to explore it more.

It looks like these last days, by exploring this, the experience of the Silence appears to 'increase'. The consciousness is absolute, and there is nothing in there. Every time, in my experience, when there is the appearance of a feeling, it is because the 'me' is back in the game. The more intense the feeling, the greater the identification with that 'me', and everything becomes sooo complicated.

One of the things that I have noticed is this emptiness in the experience through my day, the emptiness of feelings... It is not common lately to experience big emotions, and sometimes I check in, and I feel, haha, like a human! I haven't seen it that way. From the mind it looks like plain and boring, but in reality, it is life happening in a very smooth and easy way, in awe of the wonder to be at peace no matter what.

Thank you for this great adventure next to you, with your guidance and love.

Dasahara

I Love Exploring

From: Nandita, Mexico
Date: February 07, 2022

To your question Teacher:

Senses and emotions, in my experience, were all I lived, going from analysing the reasons why I was feeling WHATEVER I FELT, to blaming everything and everyone for that. Very extenuating, sad, anguishing, troubled, confused and not stable at all.

But it seems to be, to me, that in living in the now, the feeling is not predominating. The predominating state of light, of presence, has no feelings because it surpasses them. It is beyond feelings.

What is experienced as happiness is the quality of the consciousness itself. It has nothing to do with feelings. It is not a feeling. It is the pure quality of the presence of the now. Where nothing like feelings touch the state. Whenever the feelings present due to interpretations of our minds, then we continue to live in suffering and battle again, but they soon go since they are not part of consciousness itself.

So, it seems to be that we are transcending feelings to the point of no return to a life of feelings.

It is not necessary to depend on feelings, that is very risky. We can lose everything by believing that feelings are our banner of truth. They are not. Our banner of truth is void of emotions. Is feelingless.

And that does not mean that we are less human. We are

just more equilibrated or free. We are swimming in a state where feelings are gone. We are free of feelings. We feel completeness, we feel unity, we feel the now, where the fullness devoid of feelings is possible and true.

These all are just answers that come from practising Ascension and following your retreats.

Thank you, dear Teacher.

Nandita

"Does Awareness Feel?" Homework

From: Indra, United States
Date: February 07, 2022

Dear MKI,

I worked on the homework last night. Homework: Does the awareness that you are, feel?

I discovered that the emotions that did come floating through the body or nervous system did not emanate from awareness. Furthermore, anything that I appeared to own was mostly out of confusion or even more sneaky habits of mine. I.e., some of my favourite fears and desires that I hold dear when I worry about the outcome, seem to distract me more but still dissipate in the light of full consciousness.

All in all, no, the awareness that I am doesn't feel, if anything the body reacts to thoughts, but I am Pure Consciousness.

Love,

Indra

Does the Real You Have Feelings?

From: Chandan, Germany
Date: February 08, 2022

Hi Maharishi!

It seems like there needs to be a 'me', a movement away from here in order for there to be feeling. Catching that 'me' early makes feelings very, very short-lived and they appear as illusory as thoughts. And like in the case of thoughts, there seems to be a 'me' component in feeling also. But the infinite Self in its unmovingness and emptiness appears to not be involved or altered or even in relation to anything that appears. It is in a realm entirely of its own. It seems to be eternally separate from everything appearing within it, although all of it is 'it'. They don't ever touch, although they are one.

This is a cool thing to play with!!

Thank you!!

Chandan

Playing with the Homework

From: Arjuna, United Kingdom
Date: February 08, 2022

Hallo!

Your homework about whether awareness feels...

I've still been playing with it, and the only real thing I can say is that I know when I fly off the handle at the kids or something like that, I'm not choosing. When I choose, there's an instant reset and no reaction.

Right now, I'd say that awareness is full but empty. It's switched on but carrying nothing. I wouldn't say it feels. Feeling happens when I leave the space of holding nothing and zoom into the physical or emotional sensation.

I really like playing with holding nothing, being empty, zooming out from the detail of 'what next' or the latest problem.

It's still surprising how everything gets done without doing.

Is that a feeling? That surprise? Nah, probably just commentary... but whatever.

I shall keep playing.

Tons of love

Arjuna

Does Awareness Feel?

From: Nagaraj, Germany
Date: February 08, 2022

Dear Maharishi,

When you first asked this question, my gut reaction was to shout 'yes', 'absolutely', '100%'! The reason I thought awareness feels is because when I feel conscious, plugged in, in the zone, etc. I feel 100% alive. And when such an experience occurs, all my senses are cranked up to the max. I am acutely aware of all my surroundings. Colours, smells, sounds, etc. are vibrant and alive, and I feel as if I am plugged directly into the universe's power socket.

But I now also realise that pure awareness is not the experiencer but the witness. Pure awareness simply observes, without feeling, without judgment, without a desire to interfere. The body is experiencing life through the nervous system and that of course includes sensations, feelings, thoughts even. Pure awareness though is an out-of-body experience.

During a peak experience, when I am in the flow, everything is dialed up to 10. It's a fabulous experience and I often get that sensation during or just after Ascension but fundamentally that sensation is a physical experience.

Pure awareness is not physical, it is a state of consciousness where we are allowed to bear witness to creation unfolding, in all its majestic, divine beauty.

Lots of love,

Nagaraj

Being Wired and Awareness

From: Tapas, Germany
Date: February 08, 2022

Dear Maharishi,

Now, I actually sat down to share the following experiences with you…

I have been very challenged by the last chemotherapy treatment. I feel constantly wired, with no relief. I am shaking, hyperalert, and in subtle pain throughout my body, whilst not being able to keep my eyes open from tiredness.

Ascending - being so wired - can be the most challenging roller coaster ride of all. I sometimes ascend 10 times in a row for 5 minutes or so each. Whenever I feel like I am going to faint, I stop. Ascending can be overwhelming with so much going on in the body.

Now, this is the interesting part. If grace allows, regardless of all of the above, I stay razor-sharp with the awareness itself, and it's a different dance. It's the dance of such wonder and wildness. You really get to Know grace. This is awareness celebrating.

Back to your question if awareness feels. It's the homework I currently play with the most, even though I 'think' I've experienced the answer. NO. Awareness does not feel. It witnesses from the eye of the storm. Feelings are part of the movement, like emotions, thoughts, and sensations. They are amazing aids to stay alive in this time-bound body. Awareness is timeless. Awareness does not move.

With love,

Tapas

Feeling v.s. Awareness

From: Shukri Devi, United Kingdom
Date: February 10, 2022

Talking of feeling and awareness - I'm loving playing with it, because of the crystal-clear alertness it brings to the experience.

It's shining a light on whether there is a difference between an intuitive yes or no (where often there is a feeling as part of the knowing) or whether the feeling is just an opinion.

An intuitive hit or creation can often bring excitement, but any emotion which comes up lasts for a very short period of time.

Pure awareness in its purest form is exactly that, pure awareness. And sometimes things pop up within that experience which is energy within awareness. It feels as though the whole thing is given to us and happens through us. It also feels like there is so much more. I'm LOVING IT!!

Love,

Shukri

Awareness and Feeling

From: Amaraj, United Kingdom
Date: February 13, 2022

Hi Maharishi,

I have been trying to observe the relationship between awareness and feelings. I think the homework was "The pure Awareness that you are, does it feel?"

It seems that Awareness has only itself. Awareness can be aware of all sorts of things including feelings, but I see feelings as a function of the body/thinking mind. When awareness is aware of the Silence, is it any different or in any way separate from the Silence? It seems to me that it is not. There is certainly peace and stillness in the Silence. There is no sense of any desire or need required by Awareness. Is it loving? Yes, but love without any passion or excitement or need. Is there contentment? Yes, nothing else is required. But even the idea of awareness being loving or content is an idea of the mind and does not seem to be required. Awareness just is! Maybe when Awareness is being aware of itself, everything else disappears - certainly a very peaceful state.

Love,

Amaraj

Adventures

From: Sumati, United Kingdom
Date: February 10, 2022

Hi Maharishi,

Life is good. It's playful, engaging, surprising and meaningful. The connection is vibrant. There's a simplicity to the experience which I really enjoy. Bright, clear, and natural.

I've been playing with exploring whether awareness feels. My instinctive answer is no, and I haven't seen anything to contradict that yet. Awareness is aware of feelings, and sometimes there can be a lot of feelings! In this human experience, I've definitely experienced that, although not so much recently I've noticed. The only hesitation comes from remembering times when the feelings felt so overpowering that choosing anything else felt very challenging, or even impossible. At the time I found that confusing because it felt so big. But since it's not happening now, I can gain no clarity! My sense is always that it had to happen like that, and that is true of all that occurs.

The exploration at the moment seems like awareness is untouched by movement. The nature of all is to witness all of life but remain untouched. The sense of evolution comes from dropping more and more stuff to reveal the timelessness of ourselves. To allow myself to be infinite in each moment.

The adventures continue!

Sumati

Homework

From: Mati, Canada
Date: February 20, 2022

Hi Maharishi,

As for, does the Ascendant, Pure Awareness have feelings, that was tricky for me. When you asked that question, I shot my hand up. Of course, he/she does. When I am still, present in the here and now, I appreciate beauty, music, and food even more and at times I am moved by the beauty in nature. I seem to feel more peace, contentment, etc. more deeply. I guess I saw the Awareness, God experiencing life here on Earth, through me, through my senses. I understand that Awareness, God is expressing itself through me and when I am super still, I feel that presence within me in the silence and there is simply awareness devoid of movement and there are no feelings or thoughts until the mind kicks in. I have heard and read that God is love. Perhaps Love is not a feeling, but rather a state of being. So, I guess if I weigh in on this, I would say God has no feelings but is Joy, Peace, Love, etc.

By the way, I have been playing with noticing the space within me and also outside of me, like the space between trees when I walk in a park and even the space right now between me and my computer. Especially in the space between trees, in that space, at times, there is a sense of aliveness and more spaciousness in myself.

With much love and gratitude,

Mati

New Discoveries

From: Mahamati, United States
Date: January 25, 2022

Hi!

My new discovery is that when I am not attached to anything, when I am not judging anything, when I am not being or seeing myself as a person... There is nothing to feel!

Just being my real self (not a person with beliefs) allows for freedom and witnessing without feelings and the movement of emotions. The human may continue to have those grooves*, but as I stay in the seat of pure awareness, I do not experience the movement.

Sooooo cool!

Thanks and Love,

Mahamati

*__The Grooves -__ is a term we use in the Ishayas' Teaching, referring to the limiting concepts and beliefs that we've accumulated throughout our lives, which in time are engraved in our belief system and form our reality and identity in the way we perceive them.

Chapter Six

Beyond this Human Form

We invest a huge amount of attention in being a better human. There is absolutely nothing wrong with that, and it is certainly important to move towards being a better version of ourselves. Yet, this human form that we inhabit, physically, emotionally, and mentally, has a beginning and an end. It is subject to change and in a constant state of fluctuation - what we truly are is beyond that.

The focus of the Ishayas' Teaching is to discover the Self that is beyond space, time, and form. It is the Teaching that helps one to discover the eternal, divine, immortal Self, which is the true essence of everything in creation. In order to have that as a direct experience, we need to first have the willingness to let go of our identification with who we think we are - mortal human beings. Not to reject life, but to experience life fully as it is: A divine existence.

This homework is inspired by a quote from M.S.I., Maharishi Krishnananda's Teacher, "You need to be willing to let go of the notion of believing that you are human in order to wake up to your immortality."

...From Reading Ribhu Gita (So Far)

From: Govinda, United Kingdom
Date: February 09, 2022

Hi Maharishi,

A good while ago, I picked up something you mentioned along the lines of "Surrender all beliefs of being human", and I have been using it as homework.

It resonated with me at the time, and whilst I got it, using it as homework felt cerebral and without grounding.

Where is this going?

I am now about 1/3 of the way into 'reading' the Ribhu Gita*, and I am finding it an experience that is exciting / disturbing / satisfying / familiar / distant / comforting / complete.

I was walking home last night along familiar streets, and it was as if I experienced a profound sense that nothing was wrong. It seemed as though my perspective had been turned inside out or inverted, and its importance was not from 'me' looking outwards but viewing from 'all' in 'all-time and space'.

From that scale, nothing was of consequence. Nothing was happening externally. There was absolutely nothing wrong, irrespective of any perceived or imagined outcome.

And this experience didn't feel like it was a big deal, just a comfortable and easy knowingness. It was like a profound "Duh!... of course, it's that!"

Loving it.

Govinda

---

*The Ribhu Gita - or "The Song Of Sage Ribhu", is a book of Advaita-Vedanta teaching, a Teaching of non-duality, that everything is Brahman, the Absolute.

Atmarati Here

From: Atmarati, Mexico
Date: March 04, 2022

Hello Maharishi,

After watching the retreat videos*, I was inspired to explore more and more actively every day, every moment, one-pointedly.

Before watching the videos, I was having this certainty of what I am here for and this one-pointed direction to remember. But watching the videos has given me the clarity and determination to play now, not take anything seriously and, most of all, I feel that everything is here for me to remember to experience now, not just as a phrase or concept.

I take everything as an opportunity to stay still now, to actively stay witnessing all now, just now. The homework of treating everything as God** has taken on a new dimension too, because I started to pay more and more attention when you spoke about letting go of the idea you are a human. I discovered how without knowing this, I was making a lot of things about being a human and kind of keeping them in the realm of the human body. See, my husband has a joke that whenever he wants to point to God, he looks inside his shirt. He says he is not looking in the sky but inside his body. So yesterday we were joking around, and he said something about asking God for something and looked inside his shirt in the direction of his heart. I mean nothing wrong with that, but I realized how I've very subtly been having a concept of what a human is and how I was keeping 'the inside of me' as inside this little body of mine.

OH MY GOD! Maharishi it looks like there is no inside or outside of anything whatsoever, all is God, all is well, all is one.

At the same time, I feel like I want to cry recognizing this and having the chance to write these words because it's so beautiful I cannot describe it enough. There is nothing wrong with anybody, and I do not have to control anything or anybody, just love and love and love. I feel like the word 'service' has taken on a new meaning because I now have a chance to be of service in action.

I also want to share I've been recognising how much is created around the 'me' because even with the whole concept of purpose, I had so many ideas built around this it's amazing. I feel relief and at the same time an urge to just be here doing the best I can, but most of all, not take anything seriously.

Most grateful,

Atmarati

*The Retreat Videos - This homework on letting go of the belief that we are human, was recorded in a series of videos and given out to the Ishaya teachers worldwide.

**Seeing Everyone as God Homework - An approach of seeing everything and everyone in creation as all Divine and that nothing is separated from anything else.

I ain't No Human and Never Was!

From: Kali, United Kingdom
Date: March 04, 2022

Hey Maharishi... Hope this finds you well and enjoying the live retreat!

There is so much I could say and so many discoveries and reminders have resonated so deeply with me.

I have no problem with being set the task of letting go of my humanness. It's what I came here to do - I've always known that, even as a child. It really is what I came here to do. I used to reject my humanness because I didn't know how else to do it, but the game has changed. Through stillness (and the supreme acceptance that comes with it) it's all allowed to move through and disappear, despite me.

Thank goodness I have a Teacher who can keep reminding me of this. I am not a human having an experience of God, but God having (what sometimes appears to be!) an experience of being human. I want to play with that for the rest of my life (and beyond... for eternity). I will not stop.

With all love,

Kali x

Humanness

From: Rudra, United Kingdom
Date: March 07, 2022

Hi Maharishi,

I was ascending just now and at some point, there was a dropping of the idea of being a human sitting in a chair ascending - which led to an incredible expansion of the experience into infinite joy and beauty. It was like the human aspect was limiting the experience. Very cool.

I love you,

Rudra

Homework

From: Sevaka, United Kingdom
Date: March 23, 2022

Hi Maharishi,

So, to crystallise my last couple of emails to you, I really see that any suffering is only ever related to my human state. It seems that somehow this makes the choice for Silence and Stillness clearer and simpler.

Thanks and Love,

Sevaka

Hello

From: Nandasena, Mexico
Date: November 17, 2022

Hey Maharishi!!!

Teacher, there is something that appears to be happening. It's like ethereal rewards popping up from everywhere; like life is magical in abundant ways, like all pleasures are manifesting; desires fulfilling, without the dude desiring, haha.

I love being empty. I love it when this experience is manifesting. Let God experience it, not me!! It's way cooler. No humanness matters…

Hey Teacher, I love you man!

Nandasena

Human? Divine.

From: Tapas, Germany
Date: April 09, 2022

Dear Maharishi,

My senses are drunk and numb. Yet I am fully present.

My heartbeat is so irregular that it cannot be tracked. It's jumping like a wild horse. Yet I am calm. There is no fear.

I cannot sleep, yet I feel awake without worrying about being tired.

It's quite a roller coaster of wild ups and downs with the new treatment. It feels unbeknown because I allow it to be a surprise in every moment. I experience each day like an impromptu birthday party. A gift God brings to the celebration.

'We are not human, we are divine.'

That reminds me of the first time you taught me the homework in Arizona in 2014. I made such an effort. I prioritised this as my default place/state to return to. It took perhaps a year to fully experience it. And now, it's all I experience. It's like love at first sight, but then you have to put in the work to let the Love flourish.

I don't know when I stopped being human.

I only experience being divine. It startled me when you pointed out we are not human. Of course, we are not. If I was simply human, I would no longer be. God is having fun exploring. I am glad I can be out of the way as much as is 'humanly' possible.

With Love,

Tapas

Dropping Resistance

From: Atmarati, Mexico
Date: May 18, 2022

Hello Maharishi,

I wanted to share with you, that unity and the greatness of this moment, all of it is now, just now. No other place to access or to let the silence be. It is just WOW. It is simple, vast and immense. The only and most important time of life is now, and everything is in it.

At the same time, I feel there is no better way to honour my ancestors than staying here and recognising that all of us are the one and only experience of now; all of us exist just now. I am not one more in the line. We are all here now. At the same time. The 'I' cannot possess that, and it seems to me that if there is no 'me', I am nothing but this moment, aware and humble right here, surrendering and recognizing that I know nothing, let God be known, and realize God is all here now. That is my only Job.

The other day, I wondered 'How is life without thinking?' And I felt it was my active responsibility to stay aware and not follow any thoughts. I have been amazed by the thoughts I believe; they are all limiting and negative, self-defeating, and sabotaging all that I am. So, I am playing with being super aware.

When I started playing with being fully aware, I realized I have to give all my attention to the Silence and, oh my God, what bliss!

My most important job is to be here. everything else comes by itself from there.

I also play actively with realizing how much I have entertained the idea of being human. Do you know what I have discovered? I invested a lot in being a better human, so much of my energy was, or still sometimes is, in all I have learned to be as a human. Staying active and recognising the greatness, or rather, allowing myself to be more than I always believed I was. Trying to wake up this human that I thought was 'me', was perpetuating the 'someone' searching for 'something'.

However, I feel I can rest by allowing myself to be here, and by letting go of the idea of just being human, therefore giving space for grace to show itself now. At the same time, it makes me a better person right now, in this moment; a better daughter, wife, woman - a better witness of all that plays its role in this life, exactly as it is right now.

And all that is required from me is to drop resistance. To just stay here and recognize what this moment is.

Love,

Atmarati

What I'm Playing with...

From: Kali, United Kingdom
Date: July 13, 2022

Hey Maharishi!

Hope this finds you good.

I loved your latest Sunday meeting... so many new ways to hear and see what we do! Thank you.

I've been drawn to playing a lot recently with letting go of my humanness. I love that homework... it feels like any time I come across anything that I have some stickiness or resistance to in life, I apply the homework and it instantly becomes so unimportant... almost funny! Sometimes I almost feel guilty for letting things go so fast... like maybe I should hold onto them, so I make sure I don't hurt anyone or make a mistake. Funny!

It's like from this place beyond the existence of an 'I' or 'me' or 'my life', there is something so much more infinite and profound, how could any of those little life things interrupt?! Love it. I will keep playing!

Life is feeling pretty awesome. There have been a lot of endings and letting go in the last few months. It's not always been easy, but it's beautiful to see so many unexpected green shoots of opportunity and connection arising in life. Things that could not have happened if there hadn't been a clearing out beforehand. It's so marvellous how it all works so divinely.

I'm excited to see what life will bring next! With love, Kali x

Humanness

From: Rudra, United Kingdom
Date: July 30, 2022

Maharishi,

Playing with humanness, it seems that keeping an idea of being human limits us to being a certain way. Reacting, interacting 'as humans do', so not allowing much space for anything outside of that - grounded and bathing in a sea of silence, for example.

But dropping the notion of being human allows us to be much bigger and frees us from "humanness".

What I really wanted to say is that it's been such a joy to discover a kind of extra level of non-'me'-ness. It completely dismantles the idea of a little human me.

With very much love,

Rudra

Part Two

The Teaching

It is said that the path of self-realisation is like walking on something as narrow as a razor's edge. Who we truly are is so pure, so formless, so absolute that the mind can easily make it about something else and we are off believing we are something less than we are. At the same time, who we truly are is infinite, omnipotent, and omnipresent in essence, so there are what appear to be many approaches, expressions, and attributes of experiencing.

The second part of the book consists of sharing not necessarily about specific homework, but of general exploration of different aspects of Consciousness and what this Teaching has revealed to the students. From discoveries of their everyday Ascension practice to experiencing our true essence of peace, joy and happiness, to recognising the nature of Oneness.

Chapter Seven

The Ascension Practice

The daily Ascension practice is fundamental, especially in the life of an Ishaya monk. It is the key to living consistently in peace and well-being. The overall sense of life can be impacted, oftentimes quite dramatically, based on whether Ascension is being practiced regularly or not.

This chapter consists of emails sharing the everyday discoveries of the simple practice of Ascension, and how it has impacted life in general.

Good Morning!

From: Haimavati, Belgium
Date: April 23, 2023

Hello teacher!

My experience is so grounded, so easy compared to how it was before. I notice such ease with being here and letting things come through me. I noticed that I had an idea about how things would come through me, and I was controlling, editing or somehow being involved in what was coming through. But now, it doesn't matter if it is something uncomfortable or funny, it just comes out. And I notice how people respond to that purity. My relationships have never been easier or more fluid. I find drama and gossip just confusing and truly a waste of time. I am having a lot more fun!

It is so cool because all of the things that I've heard the Ishayas say over the years, how their experience is, how easy it is to be here, is now absolutely my experience and I've done nothing but close my eyes and pay attention. I am so grateful to be able to live life in this way.

With the things I find hard to let go of, my relationship has changed, too. I am much more curious to see what happens than I am drawn to engage the worry or the control. And that is new! I don't have to do anything for this either, this has just changed by itself, there is no forcing.

Lots of love,

Haimavati

The Light of Knowing

From: Philip, Sweden
Date: July 15, 2022

Dear Teacher,

When closing my eyes and ascending - it seems like I'm sitting in the beam of light by which everything is known. I love this so much. It's full of joy and peace.

Also, the attitude of "all is well" came up, and it seems to very quickly erase any judgment that paints the world black - replacing it with pure attention and appreciation.

Peace,

Philip

Resting in a Cloud

From: Jayatsena, Sweden
Date: March 06, 2022

Hello!

Today it has been as if I am sitting on a cloud. It has just been an amazing and restful day. Food, Puja* practice, qi gong, conversations, and laughter all just from this deep, deep rest. The body is heavy and light at the same time. There is just ease and lightness to everything.

So, from the last time we had a meeting, I have ascended differently. With a lot more surrender than doing. The result is, I see what an incredibly short attention span I have and also how amazingly soft and gentle the whole experience is. Just gentleness, minimal straining and effort. There are much fewer cycles of the program** but, wow, what a difference. And also, it's very fun to watch what makes me drift off. Most of the time it is general fog with a mixture of the commentator. The commentator is in the future 97% of the time. It doesn't seem scary, just planning and doing.

Love and huge gratitude for all.

Jayatsena

Puja - is a Sanskrit word, literally translated as 'Prayer'. A Puja is a thanks-giving ceremony carried out in many different spiritual traditions. The Bright Path Ishayas also have a version of the Puja ceremony, which is for giving thanks to the specific Teachers in our lineage who pass down the Truth in its purity without distortion.

The Program - The Ascension techniques (also known as the Ascension Attitudes) come in the form of sentences, which are introduced into the awareness in sequence when ascending with eyes closed. The Ishayas refer to this sequence as 'the program'.

Resting in Peace

From: Tapas, Germany
Date: August 09, 2022

Dear Maharishi,

I have just noticed I am ascending to rest in peace and not to ascend any pain or emotion away.

I am in pain right now and teary with pain, yet I am in peace.

Ascension is not a weapon to slay dragons, it's a siren song into freedom from all inner & outer perceived turbulences.

With love,

Tapas

Nothingness

From: Rudra, United Kingdom
Date: May 08, 2023

Hi Maharishi,

Ascending just now there were glimpses of a state of absolute non-personal experience. No me, no man or woman, or even human. Just awareness, like the eye of consciousness. Void of any subject or object.

Love,

Rudra

Chapter Eight

Playing with Awareness

One of the most fundamental keys in the exploration of Consciousness is Awareness. It is one thing to have a spiritual concept of something; it is a completely different thing to have an Awareness of the experience. In the Teaching of the Ishayas, we spend a lot of time exploring essentially what Awareness is and practising how to become more and more aware of the underlying reality of everything.

Where Consciousness seems to 'evolve', it isn't about gaining new experiences; the evolution of Consciousness is merely being ever-increasingly aware of what is.

What You Focus On Grows

From: Jayatsena, Sweden
Date: December 16, 2021

Hi!

So, for me, the flavour of the Teaching that has the most impact on me so far is the statement "What you focus on grows". For me, that really seems to be true. For 'good' and 'bad' things.

My awareness is precious, and it can go all over the place. However, my experience of love, light, lightness, laughter, and aliveness comes when the awareness is here and now. And it really seems to grow when I focus on it. For me, it is almost even easier to see this with things that are 'bad', when I get stuck in my head about problems, they just grow and grow. They are, as you know, very common in my work life. It really seems like they grow and get their claws in me, and I put more focus on them and think, until I remember they can be gone.

The last couple of weeks I have really played with the focus, moving my awareness to the Silence rather than the problem, and it is huge! The extra spice of Amor Fati* is really pleasant, too. It sprinkles sparkles over it all. As I shared earlier, loving the experience of the experience is beautiful.

Happy now!

Love,

Jayatsena

*__Amor Fati__ - is a stoic Teaching. Amor Fati is a Latin phrase and literally translates as "Love of Fate". It found its most explicit expression with the German philosopher Nietzsche, who made love of fate central to his works.

"My formula for greatness in a human being is amor fati: that one wants nothing to be different, not forward, not backward, not in all eternity. Not merely bear what is necessary, still less conceal it—all idealism is mendacity in the face of what is necessary—but love it." - Nietzsche, 'Ecce Homo: How One Becomes What One Is', chapter title "Why I am so clever".

Amor Fati became one of the approaches that Maharishi has his students play with in moving towards surrender and embracing Divine Will: to not merely bear what is necessary but love it.

Discovery

From: Jayendra, Norway
Date: March 24, 2022

Dang! Maharishi, I can choose not to think! I discovered it today. If I am just super aware and adamant about not letting thinking begin, I can not think. And what's left is automatically here, nowhere else! I have to think to go somewhere else, to the past or future. Thoughts are vehicles to the past or future. And if I just continuously give them back, I can't go anywhere. What a marvellous thing! I can't believe it. It makes it so obvious that I am Presence myself. It does require some effort still to be so aware, I guess because of habit, but I am excited.

Lots of love,

Jayendra

Aliveness

From: Ahimsa, Spain
Date: February 21, 2022

We are having such a good time.

I feel so lucky to be here; to exist in love and perfection as something that I discover because I write. I never experienced so much of the subjectivity of awareness, and it is truly so US that the mind can't see it, touch it or grasp it. There is no mind to do so in fact. But it's so comical when it appears as such, like a lost actor that peeks from behind the curtain while the show is ON.

What a gift to hear you SO alive. What a gift to BE so alive. What a gift to ENLIVEN other hearts with so much LIFE!!

Ahimsa

Feelings and Emotions

From: Jayatsena, Sweden
Date: May 04, 2022

Hola!

I have been watching feelings and emotions, so I don't just understand the difference intellectually. What I have discovered is that most of the time I do not pay attention to feelings or emotions. When I do, both of them seem to have thoughts as close friends. I have not seen if there is a difference in what comes first but I have noticed that the thoughts seem to have a 'me' component. Not a big surprise, but cool to see.

I had a clear experience of this today at a yoga class. It was at the end when the corpse pose* took place. My throat had a little tickle. It was like there was something tickling my throat, now that was the feeling. The thought about that was crazy though, "My body is broken". The emotions were embarrassment and annoyance over the feeling. The thought following that was, "I will make a fool of myself moving and coughing during this resting moment". I laughed at myself, embraced, and loved it all. Coughed and nothing happened. All just kept on being well.

I will keep watching this. It seems by writing, that the feeling came first, and after, a thought, then the emotion came, and then more thoughts. It is a cool exercise.

Love,

Jayatsena

*In this email, Jayatsena was playing with the Homework to observe which comes first: Do thoughts precede feelings or do feelings precede thoughts?

The Corps Pose - also known as Śvasana, is commonly seen as an essential pose at the end of every yoga routine. It is a practice of being completely relaxed while being conscious and alert.

128

Playing

From: Sumati, United Kingdom
Date: September 09, 2022

Hi Maharishi,

My experience of stillness is so captivating, it draws attention without any input from me. The alertness is effortless, and it doesn't matter if it seems to fade, the experience is still of observing. The nature of the experience is unbounded, an absolute cosmic watching that never begins or ends.

The reflection of the inner experience is continual peace.

Seeing the Divine is natural from this space. How can anything not be exactly as it should be? In this experience, I appear to be untouched by world events, yet I experience it as the true source of compassion, love and gentleness. If it's not happening here, within my awareness, there's little attraction to it.

I would describe the experience without qualities, or at least it appears to be very light, still, and restful, but at the same time, there's a sense of the infinite potential of now. The magic behind the scenes. There's a sense of holding my breath at the moment before the show starts, transfixed and ready to be amazed, yet perfectly content and complete here.

Playing in consciousness with a young family offers many chances to return to now! It's a game to be absent of me so that I can serve the moment. My kids show me, again and again, devotion, pure love, playfulness, inquisitiveness, and the chance to surrender more and more (like when the youngest peed in my bed this morning!) Embracing and loving each and every experience that comes my way is fantastic for letting go of any resistance to what's happening. It feels like the natural way to be and thus doesn't require effort. In fact, the effort is needed to fight against the flow of what's being presented! Resistance can only exist when a 'me' is in play.

Thanks for all the playing.

Love to you.

Sumati

An Excavation

From: Philip, Sweden
Date: January 18, 2023

Good morning, Maharishi,

Here is a little morning excavation:

Sometimes when excavating This experience, there almost seem to be two realities. One is 'outside', the world of form.

The other is more here towards myself. And when I excavate there, I can't seem to find anything. This is an empty 'something' with no form, shape or colour. 'I' seem to be looking out of that void. That void is silent and still, and almost solid. It's there but there's nothing in there.

It becomes clearer that in order to find the person, I have to think about the person. I have to create a person and images in my mind. Until then, there's nothing here. There's just an empty seeing that gives contrast to the 'world outside'.

So, the world outside seems to be full of stuff. And the world inside seems to be empty, silent and still.

But now that I look at it, that 'inner' space seems to penetrate this outer world as well. Looking forward to exploring more in your presence and guidance.

Lots of love,

Philip

Chapter Nine

Letting Go

Letting go is an essential part of our practice. By letting go of who we think we are, who we truly are is naturally revealed.

It doesn't require resisting or rejecting things. Letting go is simply letting that which comes and goes, come and go. When we release our attention from being fixated on controlling what is, the awareness is free to see the bigger picture; that which is permanent, that which doesn't change, that which is awareness itself.

This chapter consists of emails which share about the discoveries of letting go, and how the experience of life becomes one of flow and beauty as a result.

Discovery

From: Surya Devi, Canada
Date: May 20, 2022

Hello Maharishi,

My experience while resting in the Silence is, there is no me to hold anything, and surrender is happening by itself.

Love,

Surya Devi

One Liner

From: Tapas, Germany
Date: May 23, 2022

Dear MKI,

Something I fell across yesterday you may enjoy:

'Free-ish isn't free'.

Boom - it says it all.

With Love,

Tapas

Poofing Homework

From: Vasundhara, United Kingdom
Date: June 04, 2022

Dear Maharishi,

I am so blown away by life!

I have recently closed my business down (my ethical store on the Isle of Man). I started this business 18 years ago. For many reasons, it was time to close.

I realised I had to make huge changes to open up the space for what I wanted. To know God completely. But although I have known for a long time that it was in the highest truth to make a big change, I was so scared by it and dragged the 'data bank' around with me. What will they think of me, what about all the people that depend on it, it's a good sustainable business, it's important, what else will I do, how can I action such a huge change, how can I take away people's livelihoods, they'll hate me, the list was endless… I have had to have help with the decision-making process. I have been working with a lady who has helped me see how much I have been compromising.

It has been epic. It has taken me to the edge of so much discovery and has allowed me to see so much inner violence and 'go-to' habits of not trusting myself, not totally trusting the truth, the nugget of knowing that I rest in, that I am.

I am seeing more of the habits I have carried around. The biggest being my big special go-to thought… that I have done something wrong, it's my fault, they don't like me, etc., etc.

I love the simplicity of when I completely surrender and I am able more and more to see the difference between allowing the stuff to just be there gently, that which I thought I had to choose away from. When I just let it all be there without judgement or without trying to change it, it magically dissolves and there is nothing left but pure divinity, pure stillness.

I guess it's like your old homework of poofing*! When I accept every little bit of the experience without resisting, I poof it, it dissolves into nothingness and into the beauty of complete presence.

It is completely blowing me away.

I am breaking down all the weird ideas I have picked up along the path of awakening. I have been playing this weird game of trying to allow, trying to be with, trying to choose, trying to rest in stillness, trying to be stillness. And in the trying, I have not been fully alive with what is there, what is there for me to fully accept gracefully.

I have been an outcast my whole life and running away from really going where I need to in order to transcend it. I have played so many games, and now, finally, I see that by fully accepting this moment and what moves, nothing actually moves at all.

It's epic!

I love you so much for being such a complete inspiration.

I don't have to deviate anymore. It's all God.

So much love,

Vasundhara x

*Poofing homework - for many meditation practitioners, there is a tendency to resist the experience of thoughts or feelings. We subtly (or not so subtly) try to push away these thoughts, feelings, and sensations, particularly the ones that are uncomfortable. However, the more we try to push a certain experience away, the more it persists, because we have not really detached our attention from it; we are swimming in it by fighting it.

This homework is to practice fully watching and observing when any internal movement (especially thoughts, feelings or emotions that are particularly persistent) arises. Not to resist or reject it but put all our attention on watching it fully. When we observe the movement with our full attention, it instantly disappears. Like in the comic books, "poof!"

Letting Go

From: Ahimsa, Spain
Date: July 25, 2022

I have just experienced, (whilst I was ascending), how letting go of everything is something that is done and can be done in a moment.

Also, the gratitude again for experiencing peace, the absence of resistance, trying or controlling.

I feel so passionate to talk about the potential of healing and transformation on the planet by raising our awareness beyond the known, being this one wisdom, being one with this limitless and infinite potential.

Ahimsa

Pronoia Forever

From: Padma, Taiwan
Date: November 14, 2022

Dear Maharishi,

For the past few months, things have been speeding up even more for me to let go of what I found myself still holding onto, especially when I am aware and willing to let go. The world would turn 180 degrees for me to see the contrast - but it would be with so much love and gentleness, rather than with apparent challenges. Things changed so fast but so effortlessly. It is so obvious it is not linear. It is all about NOW - every now is a whole new universe.

While I've been practising to be empty, to surrender, just sitting in the back seat, God presents much more for me to let go, to choose, to play, to witness that I am not the do-er, to witness the magic of Consciousness and grace that is ever-flowing.

Everything in life just kept weaving into muti-layers of perfections - into just one word: WOW. I could tell you all the wonderful things that have happened, but they all just end with wow wow WOW... It seems like it is hard to wrap up some stories coz I keep playing with letting go no matter how nice things might seem to be. I learned to let go of any conclusions the mind tries to grasp. I found myself caring less and less about outcomes and how things are presented, even though they seem to be so amazing. There is more distance/space that is being created. In the space, I just know I don't need to do anything. I'm only invited to witness the show without me having to be involved.

The experiences change all the time. However, definitely, as always, the whole universe has been comprised to help me experience my highest desire. With all the other countless bonuses - more love, more space, more beauty, more gifts, more gentleness, more connections with every part of me.

Everything that has happened was always happening for me - it was always what I truly wanted. The funny thing is I don't know when I stopped asking for anything for myself or making wishes for myself since I'm simply not lacking anything. However, things just keep happening for me and they keep reminding me "Oh, yes, I would like this, too, but I forgot about it."

The Universe just has all this amazing creativity to constantly wow me.

Being in trust, in love with God, I don't know what more to ask for.

I would say I want to experience less of me and more of God - and I know this is happening because I am here on this path of wow with you and all the Ishayas.

Con fati love,

Padma

Pronoia: - describes a state of mind that is the opposite of paranoia. Pronoia is living life believing that the entire universe conspires to bring good, and only good to you always.

Coming to Love

From: Śivā, Mexico
Date: June 09, 2022

I have not come to life

to learn something, I just came to love

to enjoy serving…

I think for a second about

each of those moments where I simply love, where I simply enjoy and where I simply serve,

I see that everyone is nothing less than

full of grace…

I don't want to learn anything; my desire is to unlearn at every moment. Just fill myself with the wisdom of now, so I can continue to let everything go, everything I think I know because, in the end, the mind as a human being tends to forget.

Eternally,

Śivā

New Level of Surrender

From: Brihas, Germany
Date: April 28, 2023

Hi Maharishi,

Writing to you regularly has quite an impact. It makes my experience more gentle, the focus more clear and the me-dissolving force stronger. It feels like a new level of surrender. It is so wonderful to surrender everything. There is no need to know or control anything. I can fully enjoy the moment and put my awareness of every conscious moment inside more.

It seems like even the differences between conscious and unconscious moments are melting away. It just matters less and less what happens when I am unconscious, and I don't waste time anymore beating myself up for it. I just celebrate every moment that I become aware because it gives me the opportunity to dive deeper into the heart of God. My life becomes more and more formless, and I feel more and more at home in formlessness.

It is natural for me now to just be this alert awareness witnessing my life unfold. I am content with it, and nothing has to be any different. I can fully rest in that but at the same time, I am fully active with my attention. That is the way.

Thanks for guiding me to here.

I love you.

Brihas

Chapter Ten

Happiness

The path of awakening is joyful; it's not even a path 'to' Joy, it's a path 'of' Joy. Happiness isn't a destination, it's an inevitable quality of the journey if you are heading in the right direction.

As our Teacher says quite often: "If you want to slow your path down, try taking things seriously."

This chapter consists of emails sharing the pure joy and happiness that emerge, for no particular reason, because it's our natural way of being when we get more and more in touch with who we really are.

Still Happy

From: Ushas, Germany
Date: May 27, 2022

Dear Maharishi,

I haven't had such a shift since my Mastery*. People are so kind and friendly to me; it is almost spooky. I had been blessed with many friendly people in my life before. However, I find it striking this week. Even the salesman at the snack bar left his booth to help me carry five portions of French fries across the meadow to my family, because my niece and I couldn't have done it alone. Just like that.

I experienced so many lovely moments that I am almost starting to wonder if the third meaning of my name** was no accident as I had always thought. If it goes on much longer, I might even start to love myself.

My brother asked me what mushrooms I ate in Spain because I would be in such a good mood.

When I was swimming in the lake with my nephew yesterday, the sun was shining, the sky was blue, and my nephew was enjoying himself. I couldn't believe how lucky I was. I have always been happy and full of love in his presence. However, yesterday I asked myself how I could possibly experience so much of it.

I have this voice in my head telling me this couldn't last much longer, and it would be much better not to enjoy it too much, because it would be super hard and painful when it left, and people didn't like me that much anymore, which would only be a question of time. It sounds very true. If I bite on it, it will become true.

I had a moment this week when I was working happily in my office. Happy for no reason in particular, happy to have lovely colleagues, earn money and be able to go on holidays if I get the work done now. Then my boss entered with something. And I could really see how I habitually wanted to prepare myself to defend my position, how my awareness shrunk, my heart shut down and the happy peace bubble was about to leave. I did not want that. So, I chose to protect my peace. It was awesome.

With love,

Ushas

***The Mastery -** also known as the Mastery Of The Self Course, is the most intensive retreat that The Bright Path Ishayas offer. It is a type of Ascension Retreat that consists of a total of six months of training, often broken into chunks of one to three months at any given time. It is a fully immersive retreat experience by the end of which, most people are qualified to teach Ascension as Ishaya monks. Most teachers will also return to a Mastery environment periodically to continually deepen their practice.*

**The meaning of the name "Ushas" - Goddess of the Dawn. Dawn of Higher Truth. The Worshiped Goddess.*

Heaven on Earth

From: Devi, Mexico
Date: June 26, 2022

I wanted to share with you, Teacher... how beautiful it has been playing with my vision of Heaven on Earth. What a beautiful way to live life. Everything around me seems like an exquisite piece of art; colourful, peaceful, immovable, silent, full of grace, completely alive and at the same time still, very still. By allowing Amor Fati to play its own game, Heaven on Earth happens by itself in the most beautiful and perfect way...

Everything happens by Grace, by love.

What an amazing way to explore life, to live life, to taste the exquisiteness of this precise moment.

Love,

Devi

Our Normal State of Being

From: Nagaraj, Germany
Date: November 17, 2022

Dear Maharishi,

I wanted to share a realisation regarding being present.

The trick is not trying to be alive in the present moment but having an experience of it. Once you have tasted what it means to be truly alive, with not a single one of your senses not switched on, and an overwhelming sensation of being here, physically, mentally, emotionally, that's enough.

Just once is enough, because then you have lived. The purpose of life is not to get from start to finish but to be aware of it. And it doesn't even matter how long or how often. As long as it happens once, just once, you have lived - and from this, creation happens, just like spring happens after winter.

The carousel of life continues to turn. But isn't it so much more fun to be on the carousel rather than just witnessing it?

'Life is meant to be lived in eternal bliss…' We must find a way to have this experience. Even if it happens just one single time it will be there for us to serve as a reminder, forever, to signpost what is possible. Not just possible actually but that which should be our normal state of being.

Lots of love,

Nagaraj

Always More

From: Ishani, Mexico
Date: January 01, 2023

Hola Maharishi!

I can't believe how many things I've seen and how amazed I am by life.

I'm sure I can't remember them all.

But I've been observing so much!

I feel I'm disappearing.

Each time a little more.

It's like I don't recognize myself anymore but not in a bad way at all!!

Detached from what I used to believe or stand for.

I feel like my priorities have changed so much!!!

And there are just a few of them now. It's like I can see this life as a dream. It doesn't feel that real anymore.

Sometimes, some things do. But I know inside what's real and what's part of the game, and at the same time I can't define either of them. I can't define anything because each time is so new, alive and different.

I'm grateful to let myself be amazed every day by the little things. I'm grateful to see magic and experience magic.

The gratitude is immense and increasing.

The love has become something unexplainable but so real and grounded.

The joy has been presented to me in so many ways that now I do believe it is infinite and always surprising. I'm amazed about how many flavours joy has.

And the peace, Maharishi, I think is the most precious thing. The most valuable treasure.

I'm beyond grateful for this Teaching and for you.

I know absolutely nothing, but what this sacred Teaching, and you as my Teacher show me is something that I don't need to understand or feel the need to put into words. It's home.

It's the eternal, peaceful home.

Well, that's me lately.

I love you in all time and in all space.

Ishani

Wonder

From: Rajni, United Kingdom
Date: January 31, 2023

Hi Maharishi,

I wanted to share an experience I had last night watching my daughter at ice skating practice. She does 2 hours every Friday, an hour of ice skating and an hour of athletics.

Quite often she would lose balance, fall and get back up again and again and again. She didn't compare herself to the more athletic girls, she was in wonder of each and every moment and what it presented to her. Her eyes huge with curiosity, her smile with pure joy, her love of moving and creating new shapes with her body. I was in awe of how she gave it her all 110% and how present she was. Just watching her, I could feel my heart burst with love - it was such a profound reminder of how easy it is to just be completely immersed in the moment. The dance to come back again and again.

It reminded me of the wonder of life. The wonder in the simplest of things we do in our daily lives.

I'm so grateful for this Teaching. I'm so appreciative of the constant reminders and the commitment you have to us all. Thank you so much.

Infinite love,

Rajni

Richness of Life

From: Maitreya, United Kingdom
Date: March 24, 2023

Hi Maharishi,

Thanks for the meeting last night. The homework continues to present itself regularly, which is terrific. There is an ease and an acceptance of living that is new to me. Every day seems to be one of the best days of my life, yet its circumstances aren't particularly amazing. It is that I am able to truly enjoy them. Going for a coffee, meeting an old friend, cooking supper for my parents, it's all the best day of my life.

Love,

Maitreya

Our Highest Desires

From: Asha, Brazil
Date: April 16, 2023

It is so curious that all we look for, our highest desires are in the 'Nothingness', in what is already here, in the 'Experience' that never changes. And that the human brain focuses on all that moves, changes, has a beginning and an end. It is fascinating. The whole of humanity is looking for happiness in things, accomplishments, relationships and is frustrated and suffering. And all that we look for is in Silence. It is always right here and right now. In the 'Nothingness'.

I Love this Teaching!

Thank you.

Asha

Chapter Eleven

Oneness

Although the idea of Oneness or Unity in many spiritual traditions might have been portrayed or misunderstood as a mysterious and far-fetched state to attain, it is actually an inevitable outcome when a practice is dedicated to having the direct experience of Silence and Stillness.

This chapter consists of emails from students who are discovering the simplicity of experiencing Oneness.

Teacherrrr

From: Ahimsa, Spain
Date: March 29, 2022

Sometimes I am so happy I think I am going to explode, hahaha.

Like when I put music on in the morning and dance to the rhythm of joy.

I love you!!! I love life!!

I am having so much fun playing with everything and nothing.

Yesterday morning, I experienced that there was only one breath, one wind; not much else to say but that was so sweet and beautiful to experience.

I have seen as well how the value of life seems to be the attention and love put into what is done, whatever that is, the just doing it, without awareness, it's somehow empty or breathless.

As breath being like God's breath infusing into this realm (I didn't have a clue about that before this moment, which is coming out while writing, haha).

I love youuuuuuuu!

Ahimsa

Check in

From: Sukra Deva, Australia
Date: July 24, 2022

Hi Maharishi,

Really enjoying playing with the different homework.
What I notice the most is how it is always about exploring
consciousness and what is observed. In many ways
what I notice the most is how what I observe is an inner
experience and there is nothing outside of that experience.
It seems that there can't be. It seems impossible as what is
presented is experienced.

Whether it be a feeling like a toothache or a spontaneous
laugh as I notice something quirky. This seems to be
happening a lot. Creation seems pretty funny.

Much love always,

Sukra Deva

Sharing

From: Kalindi, Argentina
Date: June 28, 2022

Hi Teacher!

Just to share what's been happening.

I am very grateful for how the universe, life, or whatever it is, unfolds. It's fascinating.

It seems like it is a magic universe building the next stepping stone in front of my feet and leading me.

So in sync.

Sometimes I wonder why it shows me clues if I can't really do much about it. And although I sometimes can see the clues, it still surprises me.

Sometimes the clues are just clues and I don't always get them until the event passes. And sometimes they are very clear information about what is about to happen, but I still cannot do anything about it.

Also, this week, it became apparent how everything, and I mean everything, even planets, seem to be moving in sync with my experience. Like it would be only one experience, like one big being.

Of which I can only see a little part: my experience.

So amazing.

Lots of love, Kalindi

Sacredness

From: Rudra, United Kingdom
Date: January 12, 2023

Maharishi,

This morning I was walking along the road after the school drop off and there was a banal thought in my head.

At some point, awareness dawned, and presence was anchored. And with that the sense that every single aspect of that presence - the physical world, consciousness was absolutely sacred. It was grey, still dark and raining, (so not at all 'attractive') and yet all of the external evaluations melted away to give way to a specialness that was, and still is, innate in everything.

Eternal love,

Rudra

Hi Teacher...

From: Sukradev, Argentina
Date: December 6, 2022

Greetings dear Teacher.

At this moment the perception of silence is different, it is like walking in this, eating this… It shows itself as the base and origin of everything, it is only silence, there is only silence.

It goes beyond the idea of "closer than your next breath", it is showing itself to be all there is. There is nothing that is outside of this, and nothing that is not this…

It is full of silence, completely full of living silence.

I love you.

Sukradev

Emptiness

From: Śivakari, Mexico
Date: September 20, 2022

Hello Teacher!

I have been experiencing a lot of emptiness these days, not an ugly emptiness, but a nothingness, even of my identity. It seems as if instead of me being the subject living, I am the context in which life happens. I don't know if this makes sense, but it's as if it were nothing. As if it were the silence from which the sound emanates. As if it were this void where the action arises, I don't think I've ever enjoyed knowing anything so much, or wanted to know nothing... the excitement and curiosity to see what life reveals to me is great and sweet.

Śivakari

Infinity

From: Śivā, Mexico
Date: December 15, 2022

Being here, witnessing this infinite nothingness where everything is created, witnessing the creation itself.

There is so much gratitude that my heart explodes with joy.

Everything that happens, amazes me. Everything is possible, and that everything is contemplated in silence, filling every moment with peace.

Śivā

Chapter Twelve

The Path

The Ishayas' Teaching is often misunderstood as a Teaching of the Ascension practice. Certainly, the Ascension Techniques are a significant part of what we use as Ishayas and are powerful tools for developing an intimate relationship with the Silence. But they are, after all, just tools.

The Ishayas' Teaching, in its purest form, is known as the Teaching of the One. It is the Teaching that teaches there is only one thing and the appearance of others. This is not the only path that focuses on experiencing the One, but certainly one of only a few paths that do.

Our Teacher once said: "There are very few people on Earth that actually have the desire to wake up; out of those people, only a few actually want to do something to move towards it; out of those people, fewer still actually find an effective path; out of those people, very few stay on the path until it is done."

Not everyone is consciously looking for a path, yet in many respects, we are all on a path in some way. It is a tremendous blessing for one to have a desire fervent enough to manifest a path that leads to what they desire more than anything. This chapter consists of emails from Ishayas sharing their incredible gratitude for being able to have found a path and a Teacher who can guide them along the path.

My Passion for this Teaching

From: Divya, Mexico
Date: December 09, 2021

Dear Teacher,

My passion for this Teaching, and the exploration, is the union with God that is possible in this life to be able to live truly.

The power to remind humanity that they are God, that it is possible to be happy.

To live what I teach and teach what I live.

This Teaching also leads me to having more and more joy in my life, something that I never imagined.

Thank you for your support and your love.

Divya

Discovery

From: Manyu, United States
Date: December 15, 2021

Hello Maharishi,

I feel there is nothing greater or more important than discovering who you are.

There is nothing more important than searching for what is Real, what is True, and what is Eternal.

The whole of my being is dedicated and committed to healing myself and the world.

There is a huge desire to see where I can surrender even more and more to God.

To be able to recognize the perfection of Now.

And live That.

Love,

Manyu

Sacredness

From: Ishani, Mexico
Date: March 28, 2023

Hola Teacher!

I'm great.

It's like an inner fountain of pure crystalline joy bubbles from inside. And it doesn't feel like mine. It feels from and to the whole.

I love this journey; I love this path so much.

I love that you are my Teacher. Every second counts, every second feels so sacred and 'mirrory'. I feel everything shows me something, either love, peace, freedom, or clues to discover MORE.

I keep playing with awareness, it's so much fun! Honestly, it feels like a game.

It's amazing to hang out just being the Silence, enjoying the Silence, and from there functioning on this planet, talking to people, painting, doing stuff.

It feels like greater, cooler stuff is happening and I'm in service of it to do the job, hahaha.

Life feels light Maharishi.

Impersonal, but filled up with love every single day.

Sacred.

So much sacredness.

It's just that, while playing with awareness I'm discovering so much of the cool stuff, so much love, so much!! Immense freedom and lightness. The alive moment humbles me to zero.

I'm so grateful for this blessed Teaching, for the untouchable sacredness of our Teacher-Student Relationship.

I love you immensely.

Ishani

Our Practice

From: Tapas, Germany
Date: June 10, 2022

I am in love with our practice - it's so pure.

It's divinely innocent, curious, expansive, loving.

It's dancing with joy and with all that is unfolding.

It moves me to tears of love that have no words.

With gratitude that's making 'my' eternal heart sing.

Thank you!

Tapas

Love Letter

From: Asha, Brazil
Date: August 28, 2022

I have to say that every time an obstacle, a sad moment comes to me – and in my case, the sad part is the possibility of losing my beloved cat – this Teaching proves Itself. It is unbelievable how much it works. It is unbelievable how much All is Well, always.

There was a jump in my experience. A jump in 'my' Silence, in my capacity to be very attentive and aware to receive the Messages that came from everywhere. And now, much more effectively, I am able to help others in difficult times, sharing my real experience in the moment.

The amount of Purpose and Love I experience in this body sharing this Teaching everywhere, and helping everybody I can is also beyond understanding. I live in magic, I live in grace, and I owe everything to this Teaching. I also have such an amazing time ascending together and being physically together with my Ishaya Family.

Love you.

Asha

The Appearance of Time

From: Jayatsena, Sweden
Date: July 29, 2022

Hola, hej, hello!

So, I practise, and then I usually see a change. Time has passed and practise has happened. So, about 'time'... Is now infinite, and we make the appearance of time? I did an ascenders' meeting this morning and a woman shared that it was the 3-year anniversary of her partner's passing. Now she was able to celebrate the grief and love differently.

My 'progress' of ascending is happening, it feels like I let go of things and I'm more present; I study Spanish, and it feels like time and practise make me better just as with running.

Being still, there is an infinite now with every experience. Looking through the glasses of 'me' there are separate events in a linear time that have happened and will happen.

Love, love and love. To you, to the Ascendant*, to the Teaching, and to all Lighthouses out there keeping the light shining. Even in times when there seems to be total darkness, one little glimpse of light makes it not total darkness anymore.

It is so amazing. Like Chapter 2 verse 45 in the Bhagavad-Gita** with Mahesh Yogi's commentary. Introduce the opposite and it all shifts.

I know I have heard it over and over again. There have been many fun homeworks. Now, there is a different knowledge or wisdom about it, there is more applying and experiencing.

Jayatsena

The Ascendant - is a word created by the Ishayas, as a neutral term to refer to the universal force for good; the Source, the Silence, the One, God, the underlying reality of everything.

Chapter 2 verse 45 of "Maharishi Mahesh Yogi On the Bhagavad-Gita: A New Translation And Commentary with Sanskrit Text (Chapters 1-6)" - with the commentary by Maharishi Mahesh Yogi, spoke about the removal of darkness isn't by trying to find the cause of darkness in order to remove it, but to bring in light to remove darkness.

In this Moment I See

From: Atmarati, Mexico
Date: November 19, 2022

In this moment I see.

In this moment it's amazing to recognize all is alive.

In this moment it's simple to be, to be here.

In this moment I see myself in the other.

In this moment I discover all the ways, homework, phrases you use to describe the silence or show us the way, or inspire us. They are real here, they exist here.

In this moment I see all is here.

In this moment I see.

Love,

Atmarati

Seeking

From: Śivā, Mexico
Date: October 10, 2022

This constant search for the purity of the truth makes me realize that no matter where I look, who I listen to or who I talk to, the only thing that happens is that the more time I spend swimming in that infinite ocean of peace through closing my eyes and continuing to experience silence, inundating every particle of my being with the very experience of life, that is where the truth lies.

After looking for philosophers, finding books or sacred songs, they do nothing more than say exactly what I already experienced. It is as if all that exists in the physical creation in this world is just to remind me that everything is there, concentrated in silence, and reveals itself in one way or another to those who only want to confirm that they are swimming in the waters of consciousness.

And as I was in that, 'I knew it!' I also marvel at how little or nothing I know about creation. I am fascinated by the idea of enjoying that. It is not important what I think I know in the end, but by continuing to explore, there are all the possibilities that fill this life with magic.

Śivā

Watching and Enjoying!!!

From: Avya Devi, Canada
Date: January 21, 2023

"The Same Stream of Life"

"The same stream of life

that runs through my veins night and day

runs through the world and dances in rhythmic measures.

It is the same life that shoots in joy through the dust of the earth

in numberless blades of grass

and breaks into tumultuous waves of leaves and flowers.

It is the same life

that is rocked in the ocean-cradle of birth and of death,

in ebb and in flow."

- by Rabindranath Tagore, from the book "Gatanjali".

Hi my Teacher,

I just received this quote in an email and thought you would enjoy some beautiful poetry. It expresses my awe and gratitude for life… and the pure truth of oneness.

I continue to feel like I am standing still, and everything is coming to me quickly and powerfully.

I hear your message loud and clear, just "watch and enjoy".

It feels like constriction when I try getting in there and managing things.

The instant feedback loop is a blurry head for a bit until I rest back again.

I love feeling like this huge net simply has me and there can be no falling or failing.

I am relishing life and teaching… and picking an intention each day… today is Amor Fati, YAY!!!

With love and gratitude,

Avya

Finding and Discovering God

From: Divya, Mexico
Date: September 17, 2022

Hi Maharishi,

I have always known that I had something else to do in this life, always in reference to God and above all to find him.

Life led me to experience excesses until I almost ended my health, but in that walk, there was always seeking and discovering God.

This Teaching at the beginning gave me hope to survive but above all to find God.

After 18 years of practice and thanks to your guidance, I not only found God, but you have led me to be able to experience it, to live it every day of my life.

The gratitude of each morning for living and discovering more and more of this life with a smile and not with worry.

Being able to see God in everything and everyone is what this Teaching and your guidance have given me.

Peace is indescribable and it is there forever. Something that I never imagined having. Something that did not exist for me, and today it develops and becomes more intimate and permanent.

Thank you.

Divya

The Teaching

From: Śivakari, Mexico
Date: March 25, 2022

Hello Teacher!

Remembering the pure, the sacred, the powerful and the simplicity of this Teaching overwhelms my heart. Recognising that I have never been separated from anything and that freedom is not something that is achieved, but it is what I am!

I experience so much love and joy! I recognise the limitlessness of me, the vastness of God showing himself still and immovable, immutable, and eternal.

Gratitude is a very small word to explain what I experience. It is amazement. It is life. It is fullness!

Thank you, thank you, thank you, a million thanks...

Śivakari

Update

From: Rajni, United Kingdom
Date: May 2, 2023

Hi Maharishi,

So, there I was sitting with the ascenders this morning and dropping into the silence. What showed up was the eternal flame within each and every soul that continues to shine brightly. As I nourished my own internal flame in the silence, I could see it connect to other flames, and the light brightening as each connection was made - not just a few but an infinite amount of flames. Not only did the flames get brighter, the warmth more comforting, and a remembrance - it was a celebration - a celebration of life - of existing right HERE.

There have been so many moments of non-separation, easiness, aliveness, and pure loveliness of it all emanating through every cell of my body and overflowing in beautiful facets of this life. There has been no sense of time. There have been the flames of others shining so brightly and the heartbeats singing with joy in unison.

Somedays, it feels like the human body just can't take the capacity of what is possible! The expression of the silence, the stillness, the awareness is so immense it leaves the little me questioning - there couldn't possibly be more! And there always is!

I say it every time, and I'll forever say it - I've never felt so grateful, alive, innocent and wonder-FULL all rolled into one!

I LOVE THIS TEACHING! It is the teaching of the ONE - less resistance, more life!

Infinite Love,

Rajni xxx

Afterword

It is hard to find an honour greater than putting this amazing book together. It has been a long and beautiful journey. Long, because it is almost impossible to go through more than three or four of these emails without wanting to just close my eyes and go inward!

I hope that this book sparks the fire in you; to dive deeper into your existing practice, embrace life fully, or simply know that there is more. It is definitely no accident that you have picked up a book like this one. If something in here makes you excited, or uncomfortable, it is speaking to you in a language that your head might not understand but your heart knows. Follow your spark and see where it leads you.

Priya Ishaya

If you wish to know more about the Ishayas and our specific practice, you are welcome to visit our website at:

www.thebrightpath.com

Instagram: thebrightpathishayas

Facebook: thebrightpath

YouTube: @TheBrightPathIshayas

Glossary of Terms

Amor Fati - is a stoic Teaching. Amor Fati is a Latin phrase and literally translates as "Love of Fate". It found its most explicit expression with the German philosopher Nietzsche, who made love of fate central to his works.

"My formula for greatness in a human being is amor fati: that one wants nothing to be different, not forward, not backward, not in all eternity. Not merely bear what is necessary, still less conceal it—all idealism is mendacity in the face of what is necessary—but love it." - Nietzsche, 'Ecce Homo: How One Becomes What One Is', chapter title "Why I am so clever".

Amor Fati became one of the approaches that Maharishi has his students play with in moving towards surrender and embracing Divine Will: to not merely bear what is necessary but love it.

Ascending - when we practice Ascension, we are ascending. Just like meditating.

Ascendant - is a word created by the Ishayas, as a neutral term to refer to the universal force for good; the Source, the Silence, the One, God, the underlying reality of everything.

Ascenders - refers to those who choose to make Ascension their regular daily practice but have not taken on the commitment of becoming an Ishaya monk.

Ascension - is the practice, which is similar to meditation, that the Ishayas use to go inward. Ascension means to 'rise above or beyond', and in our context, it means 'to rise above or beyond the limitation of the mind'. Ascension consists of a series of techniques based on Praise, Gratitude and Love.

Ascension Attitudes - The Ascension Techniques that we use are also referred to as Ascension Attitudes. Attitudes of Praise, Gratitude and Love.

Eyes closed / eyes open ascending - Ascension can be practised with eyes open as well as eyes closed.

First Sphere - is the beginner's course to learn the Ascension practice, taught by qualified Ishaya monks.

God - in the Ishayas' Teaching this word does not have religious connotations, nor does it refer to any form of an individual living somewhere above the sky. 'God' in our Teaching can also be called by many different names - it represents the universal force for good and only the good. People have their own concepts and terms for such a force; they might call it the Universe, Source, Silence, Stillness, Awareness, Toa, Nature, Truth, the One, etc. Feel free to call it what you like and know that when you see the word 'God' in this book, you can translate it into the word that you believe represents the highest force for good.

Homework - are many different approaches, observations, inspirations, and tools that our Teacher offers as different angles to discover who we truly are and how to live life fully from there.

Ishaya - is a Sanskrit term. Ishaya literally means 'for highest Consciousness'. The Ishayas, in the context of this book, are an order of monks who dedicate their lives to discover the highest Consciousness themselves and help others who also have the desire to do so.

Maharishi – is a Sanskrit term which literally means the Great Seer or the Great Saint. Maharishi is a revered title for the Teacher in many spiritual traditions, and certainly in ours. Maharishi Krishnananda Ishaya is the Teacher of the Ishayas. You'll see him being addressed as Teacher, Maharishi, or MKI throughout the students' emails.

Puja – is a Sanskrit word, literally translated as 'Prayer'. A Puja is a thanks-giving ceremony carried out in many different spiritual traditions. The Bright Path Ishayas also have a version of the Puja ceremony, which is for giving thanks to the specific Teachers in our lineage who pass down the Truth in its purity without distortion.

Poofing homework - for many meditation practitioners, there is a tendency to resist the experience of movement. We subtly (or not so subtly) try to push away thoughts, feelings, sensations, particularly the ones that are uncomfortable. However, the more we try to push certain experiences away, the more they persist. That's because we didn't really detach our attention from it, we are swimming in it by fighting it.

The homework is to practise fully watching and observing when experiences (especially the uncomfortable ones) arise. Not to resist or reject it but put all of our attention on watching it fully. When we observe the experience of movement with our full attention, it instantly disappears. Like in the comic books, "poof!"

Stillness / Silence - There is a still, silent place within all of us. It is our natural state. A state which reveals itself when we let everything go. The context of sound is silence. The context of movement is stillness. Silence and Stillness are very common descriptions of this inner state of being.

The Bright Path - is the name of our organisation.

Acknowledgements

The biggest gratitude goes to everyone featured in this book and who graciously granted the permission for us to share the very intimate contents of their experience and exploration with the world.

Thanks to Kali, who carried out the task with me through hundreds of hours of selecting, compiling and organizing, and brought this book to fruition just when I thought it was a mission impossible.

Thanks to Ahimsa, for all the research and help she had provided along the way.

Thanks to Meera, for the tremendous proof-reading work.

Thanks to Julian, for all the legal aspects of things involved in working with fifty plus authors in one book.

Last but not least, an immense gratitude to our Teacher, Maharishi Krishnananda Ishaya. We, students, would never have the experience we are having without his constant guidance and unwavering commitment to the Teaching.

Printed in Poland
by Amazon Fulfillment
Poland Sp. z o.o., Wrocław

30944534R00114